Jayne Netley Mayhew's
CROSS STITCH
Animal Collection

Jayne Netley Mayhew's
CROSS STITCH
Animal Collection

David & Charles

For Ian, Biggles and Felix with love

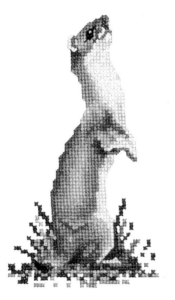

A DAVID & CHARLES BOOK

First published in the UK in 2002

Copyright © Jayne Netley Mayhew 2002
Photography and layout Copyright © David & Charles 2002

Jayne Netley Mayhew has asserted her right to be identified as author of this
work in accordance with the Copyright, Designs and Patents Act, 1988.

A catalogue record for this book is available from the British Library.

ISBN 0 7153 1132 8
Executive editor Cheryl Brown
Art editor Ali Myer
Project editing by Linda Clements
Photography by Jon Bouchier
Book design by Lisa Forrester
Printed in Italy by G. Canale & C. S.p.A.
for David & Charles
Brunel House   Newton Abbot   Devon

CONTENTS

INTRODUCTION

THIS IS MY FIFTH EMBROIDERY BOOK, which has been a real pleasure to work on as it has allowed me to bring the pages alive with many of my favourite animals. There are five themed collections, each reflecting a distinctive world habitat. The projects begin with the Safari Collection, with lions and their prey on the dusty plains of Africa. From here you are launched skyward with some of the spectacular birds that are Masters of the Air, then back to earth with Forest Creatures amid their leafy woodlands. The depths of the seas are then plumbed in Ocean Life, where you can seek out some of the fascinating inhabitants. Finally the frozen wastes of the globe are explored with a detailed look at Polar Wildlife.

Each chapter begins with a superb collage-type design, filled with a selection of creatures that inhabit that particular environment. This is followed by three additional designs, all providing a detailed picture of animal life. I have tried throughout the book to provide a wide variety of subjects to stitch – from a pair of foxes with their distinctive red coats to more unusual subjects like the jellyfish, which are stitched using only one strand of stranded cotton (floss) to make them look delicate and translucent.

The designs are suitable for stitchers of all abilities. The rhinoceros and the puma for example, although detailed and realistic portraits, are stitched using just whole cross stitch. For the more experienced stitchers there are several enjoyable challenges, like the Tawny Owl and the Little Bee-eaters, where the use of French knots and backstitch are added for extra finishing detail to the designs.

Each project has instructions for stitching, the fabric and threads you will need and is illustrated with a large colour photograph and a full-colour chart. Each chapter is completed by a Display It page, where I suggest many ideas on how to stitch and use the designs. The projects use a variety of simple stitches including cross stitch, three-quarter cross stitch, backstitch,

French knots and long stitch. These are all described at the back of the book in the Workbox chapter, which also gives you useful advice on the materials and equipment you will need, basic stitching techniques and the many ways the projects in the book can be displayed and made up.

I hope stitchers of all levels and abilities will find this book an inspiration. Not only is it crammed with fascinating and realistically portrayed animals, it also provides ideas on how to alter and adapt designs, how to change fabrics and threads, and how to alter stitches to give a whole new look to a design. Cross stitch is such an attractive and versatile stitch – all you need is a little inspiration to go with it. I wish you many, many hours of happy stitching.

Jayne Netley Mayhew.

SAFARI
COLLECTION

REFLECTING THE WARM COLOURS of the savannah, this design includes some of my favourite African animals. In the centre is the queen of the beasts, a beautiful, alert lioness framed by grasses. I was spoilt for choice when it came to choosing designs to surround her with as so many came to mind. Finally I decided on a family scene and a solitary male lion resting in the sun. Another well-known African animal and the largest, the elephant, was a definite choice. I also included two other distinctive African animals – a zebra with its attractive striped colouring and an elegant male impala head. The whole design makes a wonderfully impressive framed picture but each of the motifs works equally well stitched up on its own – see page 11, and the suggestions in Display It, page 28.

Following this main piece are three additional designs. There are cute ring-tailed lemurs from Madagascar, a young springbok perfectly at home in the grasslands, and to finish the collection, an impressive rhinoceros head.

Safari Collection

STITCH IT

Fabric:	*28 count sand Zweigart Brittney 59 x 59cm (23 x 23in)*
Threads:	*DMC stranded cotton (floss)*
Stitch count:	*209 x 209*
Design size:	*38 x 38cm (15 x 15in) approximately*
Stitches:	*Whole cross stitch, three-quarter cross stitch, backstitch, long stitch*

Prepare your fabric for work and mark the centre point (see Workbox). Follow the chart on pages 12–15, using two strands of stranded cotton (floss) for all cross stitch and working over two threads of evenweave fabric.

Work the backstitch with two strands of 310 for the details on the zebra, lioness, cubs and impala. Work the backstitch on the elephant with one strand of 648. Work the long stitches for the lioness' whiskers and eyebrows in one strand of white (shown in black on the chart for clarity).

To complete, mount and frame your picture or see Display It, page 28.

SAFARI COLLECTION THREAD LIST

1 skein each DMC stranded cotton (floss)

310	black	433	med brown golden	356	med terracotta	840	med beige brown
975	v. dk rust	3772	v. dk desert sand	831	med golden olive	648	lt beaver grey
blanc	white	434	lt brown golden	780	ultra v. dk topaz	839	dk beige brown
400	dk mahogany	3787	dk brown grey	829	v. dk golden olive	3072	v. lt beaver grey
3371	black brown	435	v. lt brown golden	781	v. dk topaz	3827	v. lt rust
300	v. dk mahogany	3022	med brown grey	844	ultra dk beaver grey	422	lt hazelnut brown
938	ultra dk coffee brown	738	v. lt tan	543	ultra v. lt beige brown	977	lt rust
945	tawny	3023	lt brown grey	645	v. dk beaver grey	3828	hazelnut brown
898	v. dk coffee brown	739	ultra v. lt tan	842	v. lt beige brown	976	med rust
951	lt tawny	3024	v. lt brown grey	646	dk beaver grey	420	dk hazelnut brown
801	dk coffee brown	712	cream	841	lt beige brown	3826	dk rust
3770	v. lt tawny	833	lt golden olive	647	med beaver grey	869	v. dk hazelnut brown

2 skeins each DMC stranded cotton (floss)

436	tan	437	lt tan

Ring-tailed Lemurs

ONE OF MY FAVOURITE ANIMALS is the ring-tailed lemur from Madagascar as they look like little bandits with their banded tails, bright eyes and pointy faces. As much at home on the ground as in the trees, they are a familiar sight strolling along in a group, their tails held high like banners. They rest, sleep and groom in groups, keeping warm with their tails wrapped around them. It is difficult to tell how many there are until the heads pop out.

The word lemur means ghost, as some lemurs have weird-sounding calls. The ring-tailed is sometimes called the cat lemur, as one of its calls sounds like the meow of a cat.

STITCH IT

Fabric:	*14 count cream Aida, 54 x 41cm (21 x 16in)*
Threads:	*DMC stranded cotton (floss) (see thread list page 27)*
Stitch count:	*180 x 110*
Design size:	*33 x 21cm (13 x 8in) approx*
Stitches:	*Whole cross stitch, French knots*

Prepare your fabric for work and mark the centre point (see Workbox). Follow the chart on pages 18/19, using two strands of stranded cotton (floss) for all cross stitch. Work the French knots in two strands of white for the eye highlights.

Mount and frame your picture to complete or see Display It, page 28.

RING-TAILED LEMURS KEY

Symbol	Code
	3047
	3046
4 4 / 4 4	524
	523
□ □ / □ □	522
▶ ▶ / ▶ ▶	520
√ √ / √ √	3024
✿ ✿	3023
	3022
m m / m m	3787
	3021
‖ ‖ / ‖ ‖	976
▲ ▲	3826
	975
✗ ✗	300
	613
∴ ∴	3864
# #	3863
◼ ◼	3862
L L / L L	3033
∴ ∴	3782
7 7 / 7 7	3032
∶ ∶	712
↑ ↑ / ↑ ↑	543
T T / T T	842
	841
⟩ ⟩	840
▲ ▲	801
▦	938
U U / U U	3371
	415
⟩ ⟩	414
◆ ◆	317
♥ ♥	413
H H / H H	3799
~ ~ / ~ ~	white
∷	310

Springbok

THIS YOUNG SPRINGBOK is just like a foal, all legs and wide-eyed. They are dependent on their mothers for six months, their sand-coloured coats helping to camouflage them on the South African plains. The springbok gets its name from its response to danger – when alarmed, it drops its head, arches its back and springs stiff-legged into the air up to two metres. At the same time a dorsal pouch lined with long white hairs is everted, displaying a prominent crest. Springbok were once numbered in millions, but were slaughtered wholesale when they came into competition with domestic animals. In recent years though they have been recovering in numbers.

STITCH IT

Fabric:	*14 count cream Aida, 43 x 44cm (17 x 17¼in)*
Threads:	*DMC stranded cotton (floss) (see thread list page 27)*
Stitch count:	*125 x 130*
Design size:	*23 x 24cm (9 x 9¼in) approx*
Stitches:	*Whole cross stitch, three-quarter cross stitch, backstitch*

Prepare your fabric for work and mark the centre point (see Workbox). Follow the chart on pages 22/23, using two strands of stranded cotton (floss) for all cross stitch. Work the backstitch in one strand of 310 for the eye and mouth details.

Mount and frame your picture to complete or see Display It, page 28.

Rhinoceros

AFTER THE ELEPHANT, the rhinoceros is the second
largest African animal. It can weigh 2,000kg and has
a reputation not to be taken lightly. Its tendency to
aggressive and bad-tempered over-reaction is caused
in part to extreme short-sightedness, though it does
have acute senses of smell and hearing. Africa has
two rhinos, the black and the white – both grey in
colour. They have two long horns but their skin is
much less folded than other rhinos and they lack
front teeth. The white rhino feeds entirely on grass,
while the rarer black rhino is a browser. This design
is easy to stitch as it has only whole cross stitch. It
uses various shades of greys and browns to give the
impression of a dusty, muddy hide.

STITCH IT

Fabric:	*14 count cream Aida 38 x 43cm (15 x 17in)*
Threads:	*DMC stranded cotton (floss) (see thread list page 27)*
Stitch count:	*100 x 126*
Design size:	*18 x 23cm (7 x 9in) approx*
Stitches:	*Whole cross stitch*

Prepare your fabric for work and mark the centre
point (see Workbox). Follow the chart on page 26,
using two strands of stranded cotton (floss) for all
the cross stitches.

Mount and frame your picture to complete or see
Display It, page 28.

RHINOCEROS KEY

317	3781	822	3782	938	3011					
413	3866	644	3032	3790	435					
3799	415	642	613	543	434	935				
white	318	640	612	842	433	3013				
310	414	801	611	841	3371	3012				

RING-TAILED LEMURS THREAD LIST
1 skein each DMC stranded cotton (floss)

310	black	414	dk silver grey	840	med beige brown	3032	med mocha brown
3863	med brown	3826	dk rust	3023	lt brown grey	524	v. lt fern green
blanc	white	415	silver grey	841	lt beige brown	3782	lt mocha brown
3864	lt brown	976	med rust	3024	v. lt brown grey	3046	med yellow beige
3799	v. dk pewter grey	3371	black brown	842	v. lt beige brown	3033	v. lt mocha brown
613	v. lt drab brown	3021	v. dk brown grey	520	dk fern green	3047	lt yellow beige
413	dk silver grey	938	ultra dk coffee brown	543	ultra v. lt beige brown	3862	dk brown
300	v. dk mahogany	3787	dk brown grey	522	fern green		
317	silver grey	801	dk coffee brown	712	cream		
975	v. dk rust	3022	med brown grey	523	lt fern green		

SPRINGBOK THREAD LIST
1 skein each DMC stranded cotton (floss)

310	black	433	med brown golden	738	v. lt tan	3045	dk yellow beige
677	v. lt golden sand	3022	med brown grey	3011	dk khaki green	931	med antique blue
blanc	white	434	lt brown golden	739	ultra v. lt tan	3828	hazelnut brown
676	lt golden sand	3787	dk brown grey	840	med beige brown	932	lt antique blue
3371	black brown	435	v. lt brown golden	712	cream	420	dk hazelnut brown
729	med golden sand	3021	v. dk brown grey	841	lt beige brown	3752	v. lt antique blue
938	ultra dk coffee brown	436	tan	3047	lt yellow beige	869	v. dk hazelnut brown
3024	v. lt brown grey	3013	lt khaki green	842	v. lt beige brown	3753	ultra v. lt antique blue
801	dk coffee brown	437	lt tan	3046	med yellow beige		
3023	lt brown grey	3012	med khaki green	543	ultra v. lt beige brown		

RHINOCEROS THREAD LIST
1 skein each DMC stranded cotton (floss)

310	black	414	dk silver grey	801	dk coffee brown	611	drab brown
613	v. lt drab brown	543	ultra lt beige brown	434	lt brown golden	935	dk avocado green
blanc	white	318	lt silver grey	640	v. dk beige grey	612	lt drab brown
3032	med mocha brown	3790	ultra dk beige grey	435	v. lt brown golden		
3799	v. dk pewter grey	415	silver grey	642	dk beige grey		
3782	lt mocha brown	938	ultra dk coffee brown	3011	dk khaki green		
413	dk silver grey	3866	beige	644	med beige grey		
841	lt beige brown	3371	black brown	3012	med khaki green		
317	silver grey	3781	dk mocha brown	822	lt beige grey		
842	v. lt beige brown	433	med brown golden	3013	lt khaki green		

DISPLAY IT

The designs in this section are wonderfully
adaptable for use on all sorts of items and can be
displayed in various ways. For example, you could
inset the male lion motif into a mug, stitching it on
a smaller count fabric such as an 18 count. Special
mugs are available from companies like Framecraft
(see Suppliers). The female lion head would make a
wonderful central image on a cushion, either on a
sand-coloured Aida or linen, or perhaps on a
contrasting blue or khaki colour. You could also use
waste canvas to stitch designs on clothing, such as
on the two smock tops shown here (see page 119
for details on using waste canvas). One smock top
is adorned with the elephant motif from the main
Safari Collection collage, while the other features
the zebra. You could stitch the designs on a wide
variety of clothing, such as sweat-shirts, blouses and
babies' bibs.

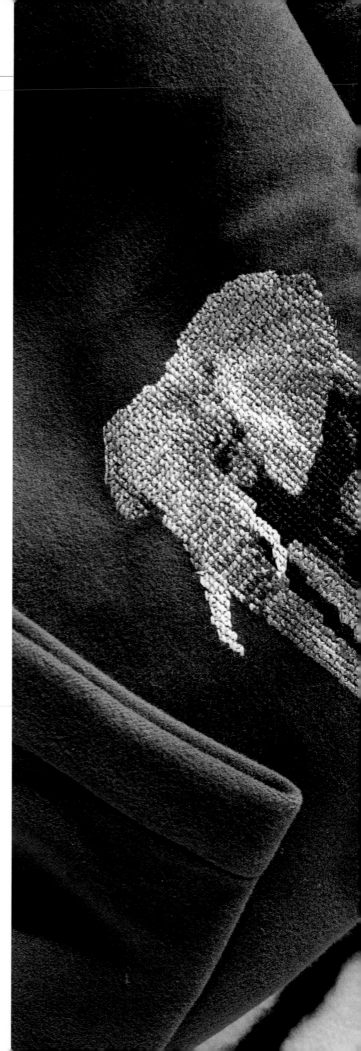

MASTERS OF THE AIR

A FABULOUS AERIAL DISPLAY opens this section, with a collection of some of my favourite birds of prey amid a cloud-covered, mountainous region. Overlooking all with a steely gaze is a magnificent golden eagle. Around him are images of a snowy owl, an eagle in flight, a hovering kestrel, two delightful tawny owl chicks and a bald eagle. I particularly enjoyed depicting the distinctive plumage of the snowy owl and the fierce eyes of the bald eagle. I included the kestrel as it is a familiar sight near my home. The collage would be most impressive stitched as a single piece or you could work the motifs singly, see page 33.

Following this main piece there are three additional designs – all masters of the air in their own way. There is a wonderfully detailed tawny owl, alert on a tree stump for a glimpse of prey. This is followed by a truly delightful study of a branch full of little bee-eaters, their emerald and orange plumage vividly depicted. Finally, there are flight portraits of blue tits and robins, showing their distinctive plumage.

Masters of the Air

STITCH IT

Fabric: 28 count ice blue Zweigart Brittney
59 x 59cm (23 x 23in)

Threads: DMC stranded cotton (floss)

Stitch count: 209 x 209

Design size: 38 x 38cm
(15 x 15in) approximately

Stitches: Whole cross stitch, three-quarter
cross stitch, backstitch, French knots

Prepare your fabric for work and mark the centre point (see Workbox). Follow the chart on pages 34–37, using two strands of stranded cotton (floss) for all cross stitch, worked over two threads of evenweave fabric.

Work the backstitches using one strand. Black 310 for the golden eagle's eye and beak, kestrel's wing, tail, breast and back feathers, snowy owl's eye and beak, the bald eagle's eyes, and the tawny owl chicks' eyes. Use 726 for the kestrel's eye and 841 for the bald eagle's beak. Work the French knots in one strand of white for the snowy owl and bald eagle eye highlights.

Mount and frame your picture to complete or see Display It, page 46.

MASTERS OF THE AIR THREAD LIST

1 skein each DMC stranded cotton (floss)

3371	black brown	3023	lt brown grey	318	lt silver grey	937	med avocado green
453	lt shell grey	977	lt rust	3768	dk grey green	920	med red copper
938	ultra dk coffee brown	3024	v. lt brown grey	415	silver grey	469	avocado green
452	med shell grey	3827	v. lt rust	3823	ultra pale yellow	921	copper
801	dk coffee brown	3051	dk green grey	762	v. lt pearl grey	470	lt avocado green
451	dk shell grey	3799	v. dk pewter grey	3042	lt silver plum	840	med beige brown
300	v. dk mahogany	3052	med green grey	725	topaz	436	tan
535	v. lt ash grey	413	dk silver grey	543	ultra v. lt beige brown	727	v. lt topaz
975	v. dk rust	928	v. lt grey green	726	lt topaz	437	lt tan
3787	dk brown grey	317	silver grey	742	lt tangerine	842	v. lt beige brown
3826	dk rust	927	lt grey green	3078	v. lt golden yellow	738	v. lt tan
3022	med brown grey	414	dk silver grey	934	black avocado green	841	lt beige brown
976	med rust	926	med grey green	919	red copper	739	ultra v. lt tan

2 skeins each DMC stranded cotton (floss)

310	black

3 skeins each DMC stranded cotton (floss)

blanc	white

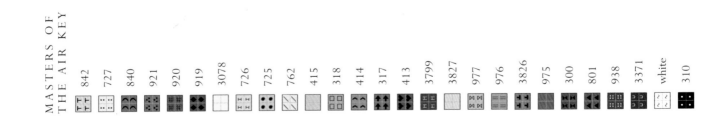

842 727 840 921 920 919 3078 726 725 762 415 318 414 317 413 3799 3827 977 976 3826 975 300 801 938 3371 white 310

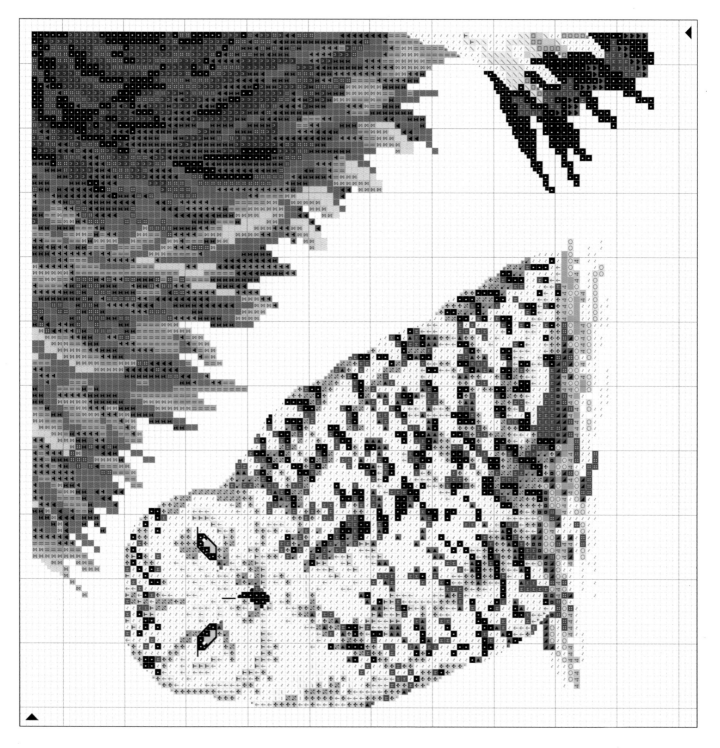

739 738 437 436 470 469 937 934 742 543 3042 3823 3768 926 927 928 3052 3051 3024 3023 3022 3787 535 451 452 453 841

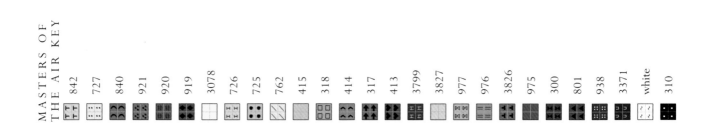

842 727 840 921 920 919 3078 726 725 762 415 318 414 317 413 3799 3827 977 976 3826 975 300 801 938 3371 white 310

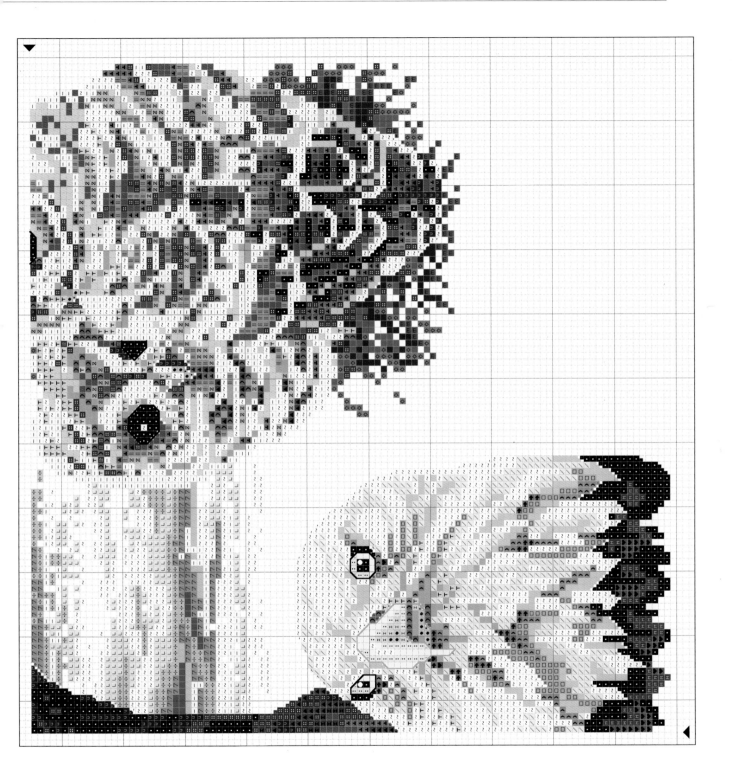

Tawny Owl

THIS IS ONE OF MY FAVOURITE OWLS, shown here perched on a tree stump covered in sulphur tuft toadstools, lichen and moss. The owl is nocturnal and can hunt in complete darkness, using only its superb hearing to locate its prey. They figure frequently in tales of witchcraft and the supernatural and were thought to have the gift of prophecy and unusual intelligence. The owl is pictured here stitched on black, with a mixture of French knots and backstitch used to give greater detail to the moss and lichen. It would look equally good stitched on sage green or sky blue.

STITCH IT

Fabric:	*14 count black Aida 41 x 47cm (16 x 18½in)*
Threads:	*DMC stranded cotton (floss)*
Stitch count:	*109 x 144*
Design size:	*21 x 27cm (8 x 10½in) approx*
Stitches:	*Whole cross stitch, three-quarter cross stitch, backstitch, French knots*

Prepare your fabric for work and mark the centre point (see Workbox). Follow the chart on pages 40/41, using two strands of stranded cotton (floss) for all cross stitch. For the lichen and moss details work backstitches and French knots, using one strand of 524 and 921. Use 310 black for the backstitch around the owl's eyes.

Mount and frame your picture to complete or see Display It, page 46.

TAWNY OWL THREAD LIST

1 skein each DMC stranded cotton (floss)

310	black	3346	dk yellow green	677	v. lt golden sand	611	drab brown
3051	dk green grey	3826	dk rust	934	black avocado green	3790	ultra dk beige grey
blanc	white	3347	med yellow green	746	off white	612	lt drab brown
3052	med green grey	976	med rust	936	v. dk avocado green	640	v. dk beige grey
3371	black brown	3829	v. dk golden sand	840	med beige brown	613	v. lt drab brown
3053	green grey	977	lt rust	469	avocado green	642	dk beige grey
938	ultra dk coffee brown	680	dk golden sand	841	lt beige brown	918	dk red copper
524	v. lt fern green	3827	v. lt rust	470	lt avocado green	644	med beige grey
801	dk coffee brown	3820	dk straw	842	v. lt beige brown	920	med copper
895	v. dk hunter green	945	tawny	471	v. lt avocado green	822	lt beige grey
300	v. dk mahogany	3821	med straw	3799	v. dk pewter grey	921	copper
3345	v. dk yellow green	676	lt golden sand	610	dk drab brown		
975	v. dk rust	3822	lt straw	413	dk silver grey		

Little Bee-eaters

THESE BEAUTIFUL, JEWEL-LIKE BIRDS are one of the most abundant of the African bee-eaters. A common bird in open country with bushes and scattered trees, they are the smallest of the bee-eaters, measuring on average a length of 16cm (6in). They are generally found in pairs or small family groups. In my design I have shown an endearing family group, huddled on a reed stem. As usual when you see a family group, there is always one odd bird sitting in the opposite direction. Do they do this for a reason, so he can watch their backs, or does he just want to be different?

STITCH IT

Fabric:	*14 count ecru Aida* *48 x 41cm (19 x 16in)*
Threads:	*DMC stranded cotton (floss)* *(see thread list page 49)*
Stitch count:	*155 x 109*
Design size:	*28 x 21cm (11 x 8in) approx*
Stitches:	*Whole cross stitch, three-quarter cross stitch, backstitch, French knots*

Prepare your fabric for work and mark the centre point (see Workbox). Follow the chart on pages 44/45, using two strands of stranded cotton (floss) for all cross stitch. Work the backstitch in one strand, using 310 black around the eyes, 453 around the beaks and 951 for the tail and wing feathers. Work the French knots for the grass seed-heads using two strands of 676 and use one strand of white for the eye highlights.

Mount and frame your picture to complete or see Display It, page 46.

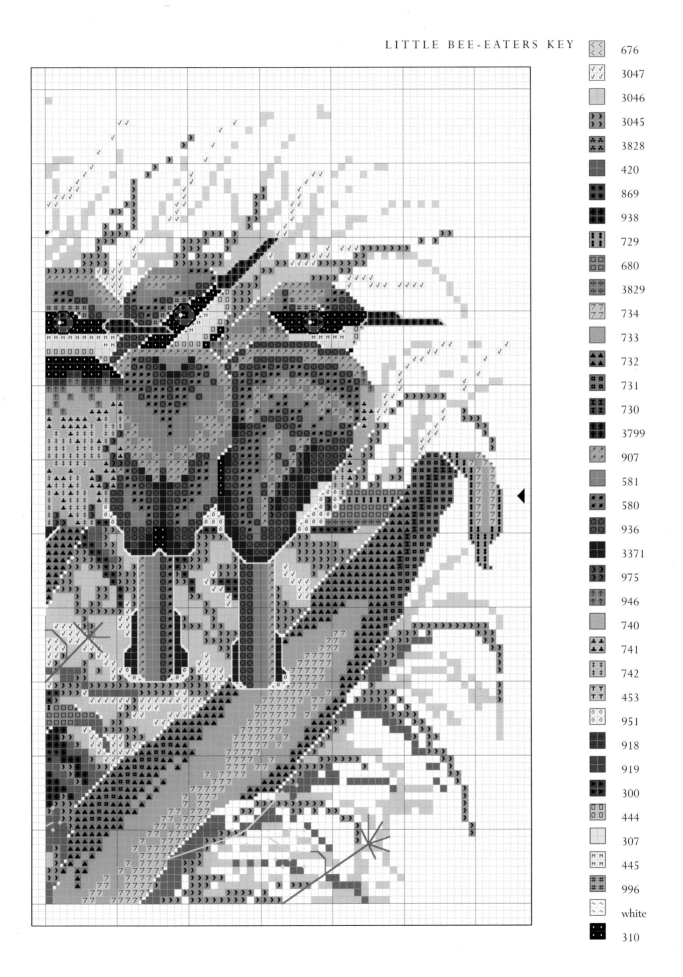

	676
	3047
	3046
	3045
	3828
	420
	869
	938
	729
	680
	3829
	734
	733
	732
	731
	730
	3799
	907
	581
	580
	936
	3371
	975
	946
	740
	741
	742
	453
	951
	918
	919
	300
	444
	307
	445
	996
	white
	310

Robin and Blue Tit

TWO OF THE MOST CHARMING garden visitors are the robin and blue tit. The robin's friendliness towards gardeners is renowned and the little bird is frequently associated with Christmas. The blue tit is a well-known visitor to anyone who has a peanut feeder in their garden. This acrobatic little bird is a great favourite of mine. In both of my designs they are shown in flight, wings outstretched. They work wonderfully as a mobile but there are any number of ways to use these lovely little designs.

STITCH IT

Fabric:	*14 count white Aida 23 x 23cm (9 x 9in)*
Threads:	*DMC stranded cotton (floss) (see thread list on page 49)*
Stitch count:	*Robin 49 x 63: Blue tit 39 x 61*
Design size:	*Robin 9 x 12cm (3½ x 4½in): Blue tit 7 x 11cm (2¾ x 4¼in)*
Stitches:	*Whole cross stitch, three-quarter cross stitch, backstitch, French knots*

Prepare your fabric for work and mark the centre point (see Workbox). Follow the chart on page 48, using two strands of stranded cotton (floss) for all cross stitch. Work all the backstitch using one strand – black 310 for the beaks and eyes and 413 for the wing and tail feathers. Work the French knots for the eye highlights in one strand of white.

The designs can be displayed as a plant stick or a mobile, or a single bird could be mounted as a picture. See also Display It, right.

To make up as a plant stick

You will need matching sewing thread and a thin stick. Take the two matching designs and stitch the two sides together, leaving a small gap in the stitching at the bottom of the body. Push a stick up though the gap and far enough in between the two layers for the embroidery to be held firmly in place.

To make up as a mobile

You will need a heavyweight interfacing, an iron, some white or invisible sewing thread and a hoop or branch. There are four birds on the mobile (eight designs in total). Start by placing the interfacing neatly over the embroidery, put a damp cloth over the designs and press with an iron. When the interfacing has bonded to both sides, trim the fabric to within 2.5cm (1in) of the design. Do not trim all the excess fabric at this stage. Now stitch the two sides together, sewing through both designs as close to the stitching as possible, with white or invisible sewing thread, matching up each side stitch by stitch. Trim away all the excess fabric, as close as possible to the stitching, to within one stitch from the edge of the design. String each embroidery with variable lengths of invisible thread and attach to a hoop or branch at intervals.

DISPLAY IT

The attractive designs in this section can be made up in a multitude of ways. For example, you could use a single robin or blue tit mounted into a teapot or

coffeepot stand. If stitched on a smaller count fabric, such as an 18 count, these birds could also be inset into mugs or cards. By using waste canvas many of the designs could be stitched on clothing. The beautiful little bee-eaters could be made up into a wonderful rectangular cushion, with a frilled or braided edge (see page 124 for instructions).

The tawny owl would make a wonderful doorstop, stitched up on a 10 count fabric to make him a little larger (see page 125 for instructions). Remember, if you alter the count, you will need different amounts of fabric and threads. On a 10 count I would use three strands of stranded cotton (floss); on an 18 count I would use one strand.

FOREST CREATURES

A WONDERFUL MIXTURE OF ANIMALS, large and small, make up the collection of designs in this picture. The central portrait is of a magnificent brown bear, the water foaming around him as he fishes for salmon. Surrounding him are two delightful young bear cubs and the lovely doe-eyed head of a roe deer. There is also a bright-eyed stoat, a fierce little mammal. His black-tipped tail is one of the features that tells him apart from the weasel – see his portrait on page 53. A brightly coloured greater spotted woodpecker also features in the design and yet another little bandit, the racoon, who is as much at home now in a town as he is the forest.

The other three designs that make up this forest collection are a beautiful young puma padding softly forwards, and two lovely foxes just emerging from a hedge of grasses. To finish, there is a regal looking red stag with a valley scene behind him.

Forest Creatures

Prepare your fabric for work and mark the centre point (see Workbox). Follow the chart on pages 54–57, using two strands of stranded cotton (floss) for all cross stitch, worked over two threads of evenweave fabric.

Work the backstitches in one strand of black 310 stranded cotton (floss) for the brown bear's eye, stoat's eye, roe deer's eye and greater spotted woodpecker's eye. Work the French knots in one strand of white for the eye highlights on the stoat, roe deer, greater spotted woodpecker and racoon.

Mount and frame your picture to complete or see Display It, page 70.

STITCH IT

Fabric:	28 count sage green Zweigart Brittney 59 x 59cm (23 x 23in)
Threads:	DMC stranded cotton (floss)
Stitch count:	209 x 209
Design size:	38 x 38cm (15 x 15in) approx
Stitches:	Whole cross stitch, three-quarter cross stitch, backstitch, French knots

FOREST CREATURES THREAD LIST

1 skein each DMC stranded cotton (floss)

310	black	976	med rust	318	lt silver grey	3782	lt mocha brown
502	blue green	437	lt tan	951	lt tawny	3823	ultra pale yellow
3371	black brown	977	lt rust	415	silver grey	3032	med mocha brown
501	dk blue green	738	v. lt tan	934	black avocado green	732	olive green
938	ultra dk coffee brown	3827	v. lt rust	762	v. lt silver grey	3781	dk mocha brown
500	v. dk blue green	739	ultra v. lt tan	937	med avocado green	733	med olive green
898	v. dk coffee brown	838	v. dk beige brown	869	v. dk hazelnut brown	610	dk drab brown
3790	ultra dk beige grey	746	off white	470	lt avocado green	734	lt olive green
801	dk coffee brown	839	dk beige brown	420	dk hazelnut brown	611	drab brown
632	ultra v. dk desert sand	3799	v. dk pewter grey	817	v. dk coral red	775	v. lt baby blue
433	med brown golden	840	med beige brown	3828	hazelnut brown	612	lt drab brown
300	v. dk mahogany	413	dk silver grey	349	dk peach	504	lt blue green
434	lt brown golden	841	lt beige brown	422	lt hazelnut brown	613	v. lt drab brown
975	v. dk rust	317	silver grey	815	med garnet	3813	lt blue green
435	v. lt brown golden	842	v. lt beige brown	676	lt golden sand	3033	v. lt mocha brown
3826	dk rust	414	dk silver grey	822	lt beige grey	503	med blue green
436	tan	543	ultra v. lt beige brown	677	v. lt golden sand	644	med beige grey

2 skeins each DMC stranded cotton (floss)

blanc	white

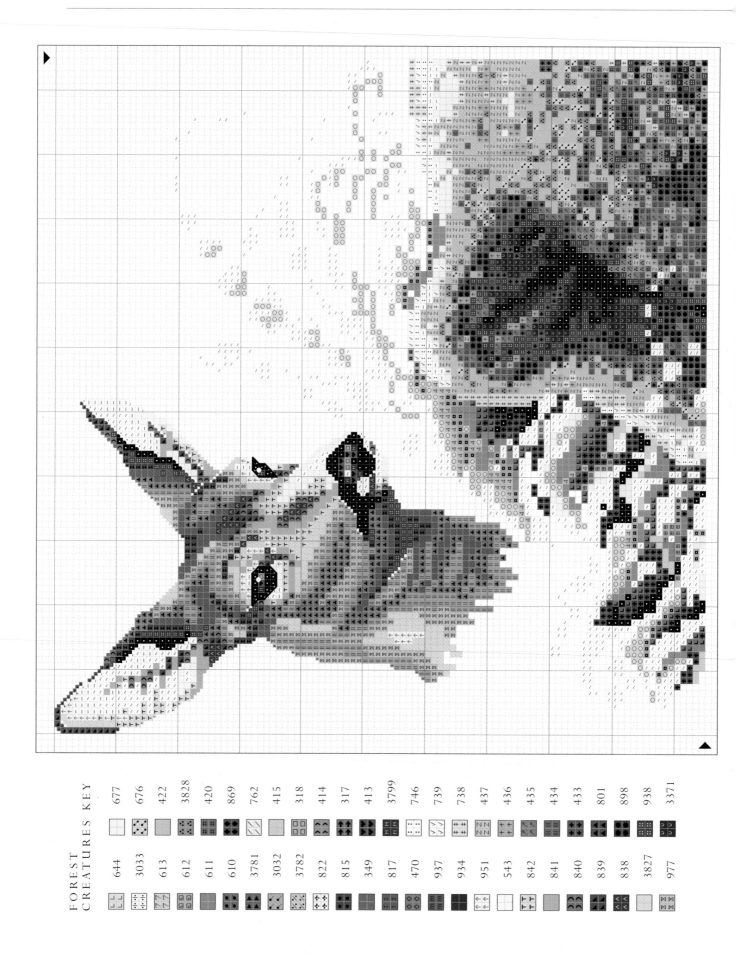

FOREST CREATURES KEY

677	676	422	3828	420	869	762	415	318	414	317	413	3799	746	739	738	437	436	435	434	433	801	898	938	3371

644	3033	613	612	611	610	3781	3032	3782	822	815	349	817	470	937	934	951	543	842	841	840	839	838	3827	977

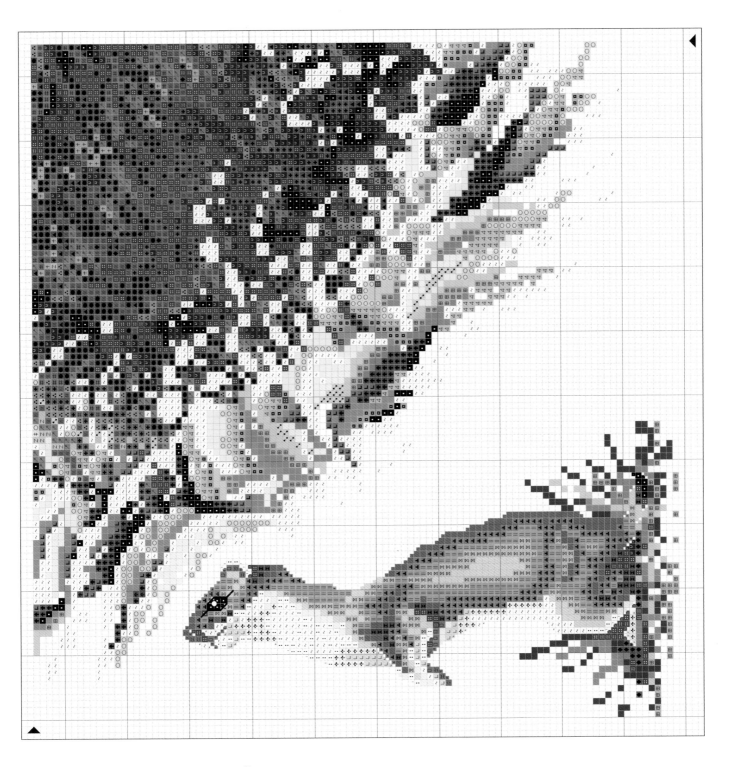

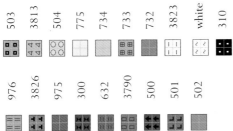

| 677 | 676 | 422 | 3828 | 420 | 869 | 762 | 415 | 318 | 414 | 317 | 413 | 3799 | 746 | 739 | 738 | 437 | 436 | 435 | 434 | 433 | 801 | 898 | 938 | 3371 |

| 644 | 3033 | 613 | 612 | 611 | 610 | 3781 | 3032 | 3782 | 822 | 815 | 349 | 817 | 470 | 937 | 934 | 951 | 543 | 842 | 841 | 840 | 839 | 838 | 3827 | 977 |

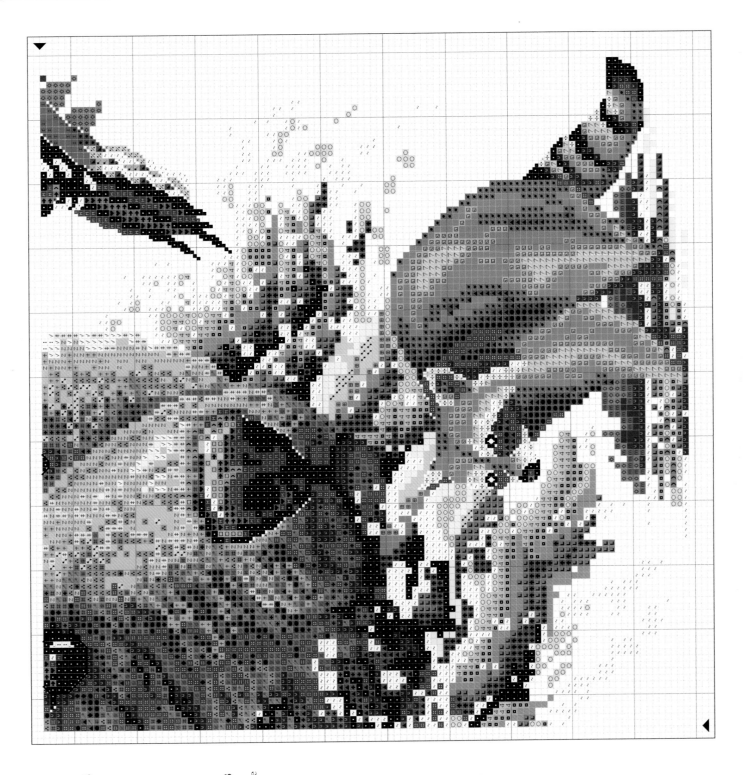

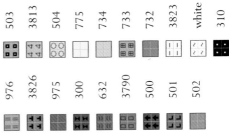

Puma

ONE OF THE MOST LOVELY of the big cats, the puma, ranges far and wide over the world and is also known as mountain lion or cougar. As a general rule, pumas are bigger in the colder parts of their range and smaller in the tropics, but are equally at home in the desert or above the snow line. Pumas have always been notable for their generally neutral attitude to man. If captured when young, they are easily tamed. Like domestic cats, they can amuse themselves for hours with balls of wool and toys, and they will purr when petted.

STITCH IT

Fabric:	*14 count white Aida 41 x 48cm (16 x 19in)*
Threads:	*DMC stranded cotton (floss) (see thread list page 69)*
Stitch count:	*105 x 150*
Design size:	*21 x 28cm (8 x 11in) approx*
Stitches:	*Whole cross stitch, long stitch*

Prepare your fabric for work and mark the centre point (see Workbox). Follow the chart on pages 60/61, using two strands of stranded cotton (floss) for all cross stitch. Work the long stitches for the whiskers using one strand of white (shown in black on the chart for clarity).

Mount and frame your picture to complete or see Display It, page 70.

PUMA
KEY

612 611 610 783 782 780 734 733 732 730 772 3348 3347 3346 3345 895 934 422 3828 420 822 644 642

640 3790 3031 351 352 353 3864 3863 3862 746 677 676 739 738 437 436 435 434 433 801 938 3371 white 310

Foxes

FOXES NEVER CEASE TO AMAZE ME: they now are as common living in town as in the countryside. They appear all over the world from the arctic to the desert, surviving in the harshest of environments. I have spent many happy hours watching these adorable animals. In this design I have an adult in the foreground emerging from a grassy bank with one of her fully grown cubs looking as if he wants to race ahead.

STITCH IT

Fabric:	*14 count khaki Aida 41 x 54cm (16 x 21in)*
Threads:	*DMC stranded cotton (floss) (see thread list page 69)*
Stitch count:	*110 x 180*
Design size:	*21 x 33cm (8 x 13in) approx*
Stitches:	*Whole cross stitch, three-quarter cross stitch, backstitch*

Prepare your fabric for work and mark the centre point (see Workbox). Follow the chart on pages 64/65, using two strands of stranded cotton (floss) for all cross stitch. Work the grass stem backstitches in one strand of 898.

Mount and frame your picture to complete or see Display It, page 70.

Red Stag

THIS DESIGN SHOWS a handsome red stag standing proudly in his valley. For most of the year the stags live apart from the hinds (females), occupying a well-defined territory. They shed their antlers in the spring. New antlers soon sprout and are fully grown, bearing up to twelve points, by autumn. Shortly after this the stag will round up the hinds to mate with them, guarding them carefully when any other stag comes too close.

Prepare your fabric for work and mark the centre point (see Workbox). Follow the chart on page 68, using two strands of stranded cotton (floss) for all cross stitch. Work the French knots in one strand of white for the eye highlights.

Mount and frame your picture to complete or see Display It, page 70.

STITCH IT

Fabric:	*14 count sky blue Aida 38 x 42cm (15 x 16½in)*
Threads:	*DMC stranded cotton (floss) (see thread list on page 69)*
Stitch count:	*100 x 115*
Design size:	*19 x 22cm (7 x 8½in) approx*
Stitches:	*Whole cross stitch, three-quarter cross stitch, French knots*

▲▲	801	⊞⊞	3864	⊞⊞	3799		772	^^	935	⋮⋮	833	⊠⊠	471
⋮⋮	938	◆◆	3863	−−	746	⊠⊠	3051	■■	3345		834	‖‖	472
⊡⊡	3371		3862		677		3052		3346		3790		
∼∼	white	√√	739	⋮⋮	422	LL	3053	44	3347		932		
■■	310	‡‡	738		3828	↔↔	317	OO	3348	⋮⋮	3753		RED STAG KEY

PUMA THREAD LIST
1 skein each DMC stranded cotton (floss)

310	black	434	lt brown golden	676	lt golden sand	353	v. lt peach
642	dk beige grey	934	black avocado green	772	v. lt yellow green	782	dk topaz
blanc	white	435	v. lt brown golden	677	v. lt golden sand	352	lt peach
644	med beige grey	895	v. dk hunter green	730	v. dk olive green	783	med topaz
3371	black brown	436	tan	746	off white	351	peach
822	lt beige grey	3345	v. dk yellow green	732	olive green	610	dk drab brown
938	ultra dk coffee brown	437	lt tan	3862	dk brown	3031	v. dk mocha brown
420	dk hazelnut brown	3346	dk yellow green	733	med olive green	611	drab brown
801	dk coffee brown	738	v. lt tan	3863	med brown	3790	ultra dk beige brown
3828	hazelnut brown	3347	med yellow green	734	lt olive green	612	lt drab brown
433	med brown golden	739	ultra v. lt tan	3864	lt brown	640	v. dk beige grey
422	lt hazelnut brown	3348	lt yellow green	780	ultra v. dk topaz		

FOXES THREAD LIST
1 skein each DMC stranded cotton (floss)

310	black	543	ultra v. lt beige brown	3827	v. lt rust	832	golden olive
838	v. dk beige brown	300	v. dk mahogany	469	avocado green	414	dk silver grey
blanc	white	434	lt brown golden	945	tawny	833	lt golden olive
839	dk beige brown	975	v. dk rust	470	lt avocado green	676	lt golden sand
3371	black brown	435	v. lt brown golden	951	lt tawny	780	ultra v. dk topaz
840	med beige brown	3826	dk rust	471	v. lt avocado green	677	v. lt golden sand
938	ultra dk coffee brown	436	tan	3799	v. dk pewter grey	782	dk topaz
841	lt beige brown	976	med rust	829	v. dk golden olive	746	off white
898	v. dk coffee brown	934	black avocado green	413	dk silver grey	783	med topaz
842	v. lt beige brown	977	lt rust	831	med golden olive		
801	dk coffee brown	937	med avocado green	317	silver grey		

RED STAG THREAD LIST
1 skein each DMC stranded cotton (floss)

310	black	801	dk coffee brown	3863	med brown	677	v. lt golden sand
3053	green grey	3348	lt yellow green	935	dk avocado green	834	v. lt golden olive
blanc	white	738	v. lt tan	3864	lt brown	746	off white
3052	med green grey	3347	med yellow green	3753	ultra v. lt antique blue	833	lt golden olive
3371	black brown	739	ultra v. lt tan	3828	hazelnut brown	3799	v. dk pewter grey
3051	dk green grey	3346	dk yellow green	932	lt antique blue	472	ultra lt avocado green
938	ultra dk coffee brown	3862	dk brown	422	lt hazelnut brown	317	silver grey
772	v. lt yellow green	3345	v. dk yellow green	3790	ultra dk beige grey	471	v. lt avocado green

DISPLAY IT

There are some lovely designs in this section, perfect for use on all sorts of items. The main Forest Creatures design could be made up into an impressive square cushion, while the handsome foxes would make a wonderful rectangular cushion (see page 124 for instructions). To give an added dimension in the foxes design, the cross stitches of the grass seed-heads could be replaced with similarly coloured French knots or beads. The roe deer head and the stoat would make lovely small pictures. The puma would look wonderful stitched up into a doorstop on a 10 count Aida fabric (see page 125 for instructions) or could be stitched on canvas in a larger count for a superb rug or wall hanging (see pages 119 and 126 for instructions). If you stitch the design on canvas, remember to choose a complementary colour wool (yarn) to fill the background.

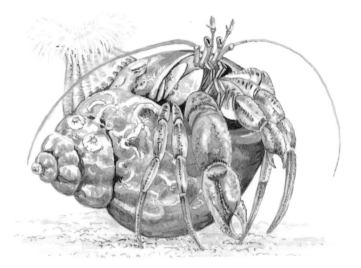

OCEAN LIFE

A WONDERFUL DOLPHIN is the central motif for this
opening design for life in the ocean. I had such a
wide variety to choose from, that I decided in the end
on a mixture of large and small. The largest is the
whale shark, a beautiful, plankton eater that little is
known about. The smallest is the hermit crab: as he
grows he finds a vacant shell and moves in as fast as
he can, as this is when he is most vulnerable. A group
of dolphins leaping joyfully, and a small shoal of
tropical blue-lined snappers add movement to the
design. Three delicate jellyfish round off the
collection. To make the jellyfish look more delicate,
they are stitched with only one strand of stranded
cotton (floss).

The three other designs that make up the ocean life
collection are quite unusual and versatile – see
Display It on page 92 for just a few ideas. There is a
mass of baby turtles emerging from the sand, then an
abstract design of a shoal of mackerel, and to finish a
magnificent humpback whale and calf.

Ocean Life

STITCH IT

Fabric:	*28 count blue Zweigart Brittney 59 x 59cm (23 x 23in)*
Threads:	*DMC stranded cotton (floss)*
Stitch count:	*209 x 209*
Design size:	*38 x 38cm (15 x 15in) approx*
Stitches:	*Whole cross stitch, three-quarter cross stitch, backstitch, French knots*

Prepare your fabric for work and mark the centre point (see Workbox). Follow the chart on pages 76–79, working over two threads of evenweave fabric, using two strands of stranded cotton (floss) for all the cross stitch except the jellyfish which is worked with one strand.

Work all the backstitches with one strand. Use black 310 for the main dolphin's mouth and the hermit crab's eyes. Use 3799 around the bodies of the dolphin group. Use 535 for the eyes and mouths of the shoal of fish and 3750 for the body stripes. Use 3046 and 3045 for the jellyfish tendrils. Work the French knots with two strands of white for the eye highlights on the fish shoal and the hermit crab.

Mount and frame your picture to complete or see Display It, page 92.

OCEAN LIFE THREAD LIST
1 skein each DMC stranded cotton (floss)

310	black	762	v. lt pearl grey	775	v. lt baby blue	519	sky blue
725	topaz	370	med mustard	975	v. dk rust	3045	dk yellow beige
3799	v. dk pewter grey	3750	v. dk antique blue	3809	v. dk turquoise	3761	lt sky blue
800	pale delft blue	371	mustard	801	dk coffee brown	3756	ultra v. lt baby blue
413	dk silver grey	930	dk antique blue	3810	dk turquoise	ecru	ecru
809	delft blue	372	lt mustard	938	ultra dk coffee brown	928	v. lt grey green
317	silver grey	931	med antique blue	939	v. dk navy blue	3078	v. lt golden yellow
453	lt shell grey	3827	v. lt rust	738	v. lt tan	927	lt grey green
414	dk silver grey	932	lt antique blue	517	dk wedgewood	727	v. lt topaz
452	med shell grey	977	lt rust	437	lt tan	729	med golden sand
318	lt silver grey	3752	v. lt antique blue	3760	med wedgewood	726	lt topaz
451	dk shell grey	976	med rust	3047	lt yellow beige		
415	silver grey	3753	ultra v. lt antique blue	518	lt wedgewood		
535	v. lt ash grey	3826	dk rust	3046	med yellow beige		

2 skeins each DMC stranded cotton (floss)

blanc	white

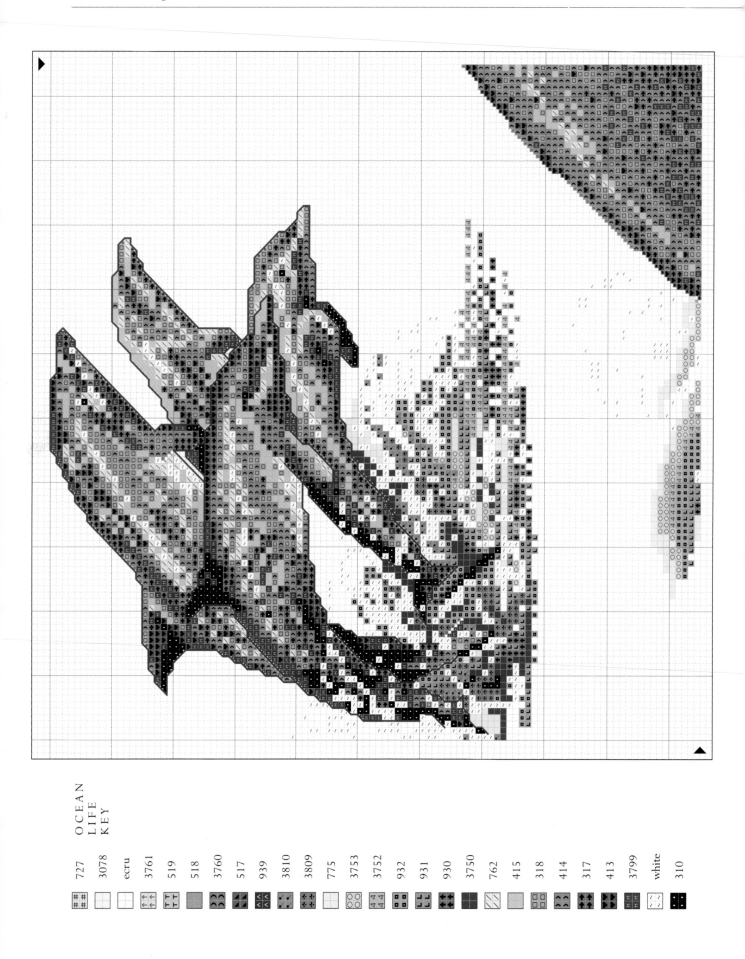

OCEAN
LIFE
KEY

727   3078   ecru   3761   519   518   3760   517   939   3810   3809   775   3753   3752   932   931   930   3750   762   415   318   414   317   413   3799   white   310

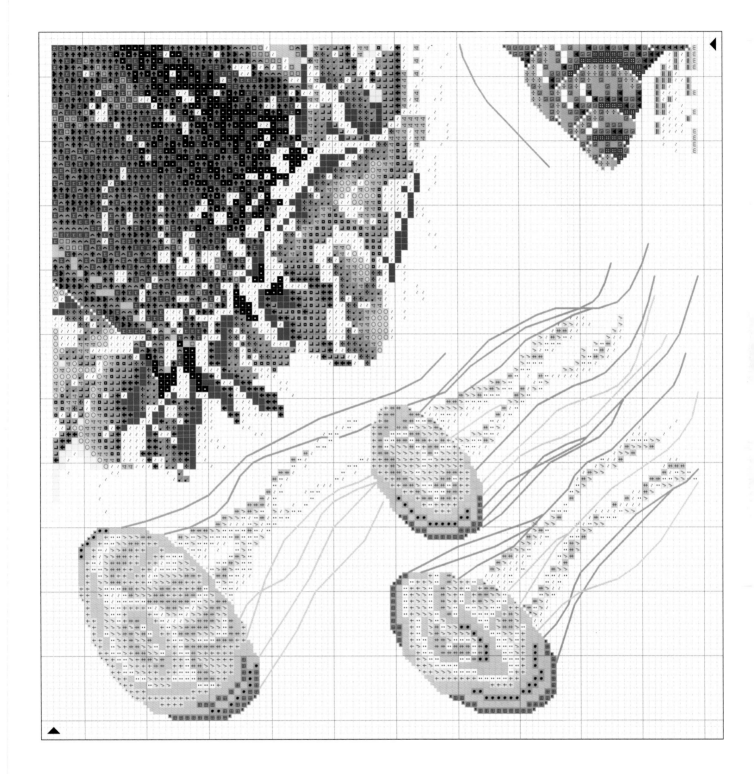

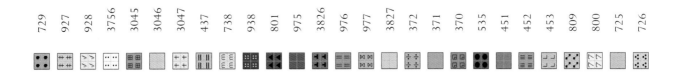

729 927 928 3756 3045 3046 3047 437 738 938 801 975 3826 976 977 3827 372 371 370 535 451 452 453 809 800 725 726

Baby Turtles

THIS UTTERLY DELIGHTFUL heap of baby turtles emerging from the sand after hatching are beginning their mad rush to the sea and hopefully to survival. So many are born but with so many hazards to overcome, very few survive. This design is very versatile, as it can be stitched as a whole or you can take a portion of it and use it to decorate a towel border. The blue arrows on the chart indicate the border width when using the design for an Aida band (see page 119 for using embroidery bands).

STITCH IT

Fabric:	*14 count white Aida 48 x 41cm (18¾ x16¼in)*
Threads:	*DMC stranded cotton (floss) (see thread list page 91)*
Stitch count:	*150 x 110*
Design size:	*27 x 20cm (10¾ x 8in) approx*
Stitches:	*Whole cross stitch, three-quarter cross stitch, backstitch*

Prepare your fabric for work and mark the centre point (see Workbox). Follow the chart on pages 82/83, using two strands of stranded cotton (floss) for all cross stitch. Work the 3799 backstitch in one strand of stranded cotton (floss).

Mount and frame your picture to complete or see Display It, page 92.

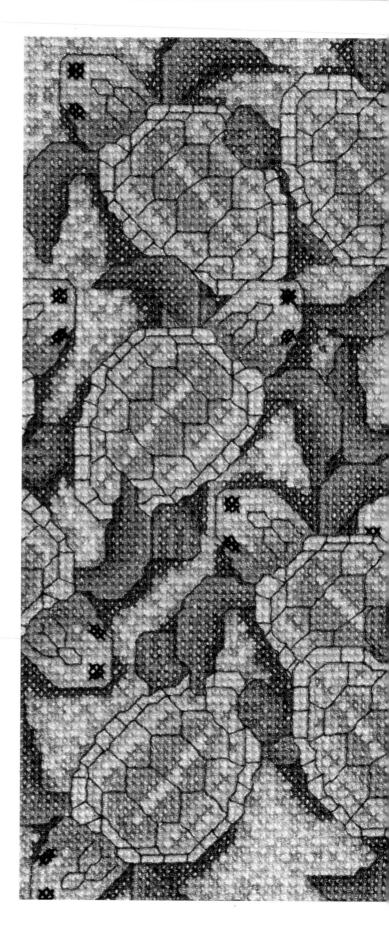

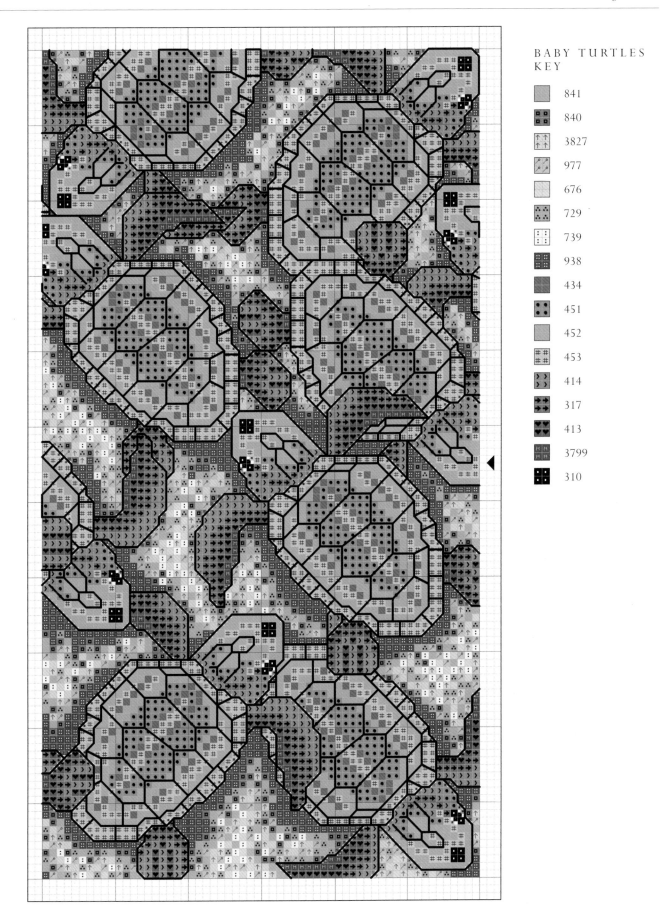

BABY TURTLES
KEY

	841
	840
	3827
	977
	676
	729
	739
	938
	434
	451
	452
	453
	414
	317
	413
	3799
	310

Mackerel Shoal

MACKEREL WERE MY INSPIRATION for this design with their gorgeous colouring. A mass of fish makes this composition quite abstract. As with the turtles, this design is versatile and can be used whole or in part, for example as a towel border. The blue arrows on the chart refer to the border width when using the design for an Aida band (see page 119 for using embroidery bands).

STITCH IT

Fabric:	*14 count white Aida 48 x 41cm (18¾ x 16in)*
Threads:	*DMC stranded cotton (floss) (see thread list page 91)*
Stitch count:	*150 x 110*
Design size:	*27 x 20cm (10¾ x 8in) approx*
Stitches:	*Whole cross stitch*

Prepare your fabric for work and mark the centre point (see Workbox). Follow the chart on pages 86/87, using two strands of stranded cotton (floss) for all cross stitch.

Mount and frame your picture to complete or see Display It, page 92.

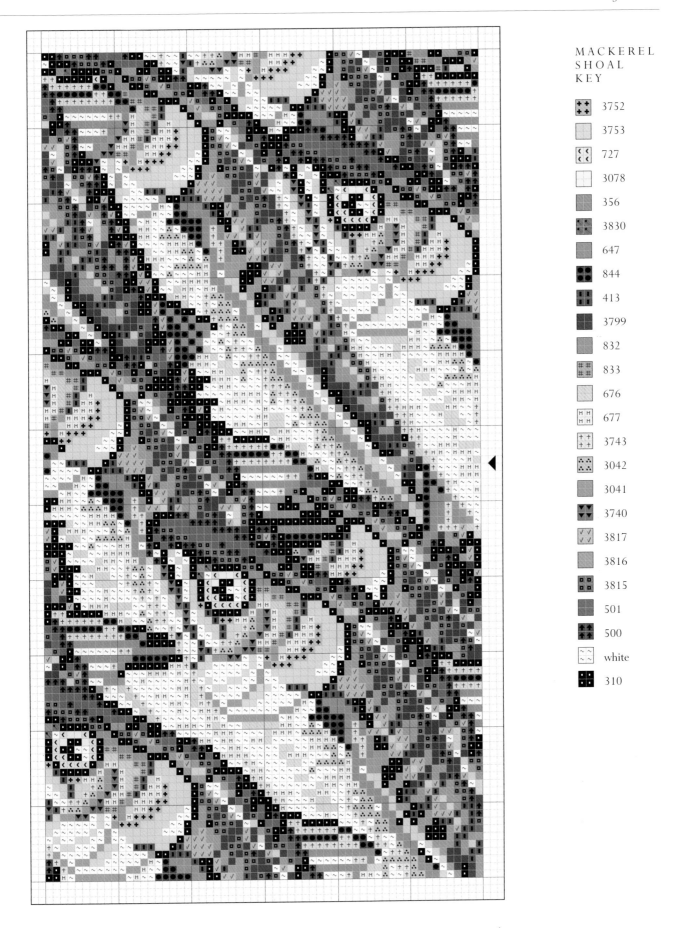

MACKEREL
SHOAL
KEY

Symbol	Code
✛✛	3752
▦	3753
⟨⟨	727
□	3078
▨	356
⁘	3830
▨	647
⬤⬤	844
▮▮	413
▩	3799
▨	832
＃＃	833
▨	676
нн	677
✛✛	3743
⁖⁖	3042
▨	3041
▼▼	3740
√√	3817
▨	3816
▫▫	3815
▨	501
⬆⬆	500
~~	white
▪▪	310

Humpback Whale and Calf

THIS MAGNIFICENT HUMPBACK WHALE and calf are shown
here stitched on cadet blue Aida to imply the ocean
depths, with air bubbles trailing behind them as they dive
down from the surface. An adult whale can weigh up to
forty tons. The creature is also remarkable for its
extremely long flippers, which can be up to a third of its
body length. Humpback whales assemble each year
around the Hawaiian Islands to breed. After giving birth,
mating and their wonderful bouts of singing, the whales
then return to the seas off Alaska to feed on krill.

STITCH IT

Fabric:	*14 count cadet blue Aida*
	38 x 37cm (15 x 14½in)
Threads:	*DMC stranded cotton (floss)*
	(see thread list page 91)
Stitch count:	*100 x 92*
Design size:	*18 x 17cm (7 x 6½in) approx*
Stitches:	*Whole cross stitch,*
	three-quarter cross stitch

Prepare your fabric for work and mark the centre point (see Workbox). Follow the
chart on page 90, using two strands of stranded cotton (floss) for all cross stitch. If
preferred, you can use beads or French knots to replace all the white cross stitches.
If you do use beads, choose a colour that matches or is complementary to the thread
colour you are replacing (see Adding Beads page 118).

Mount and frame your picture to complete or see Display It, page 92.

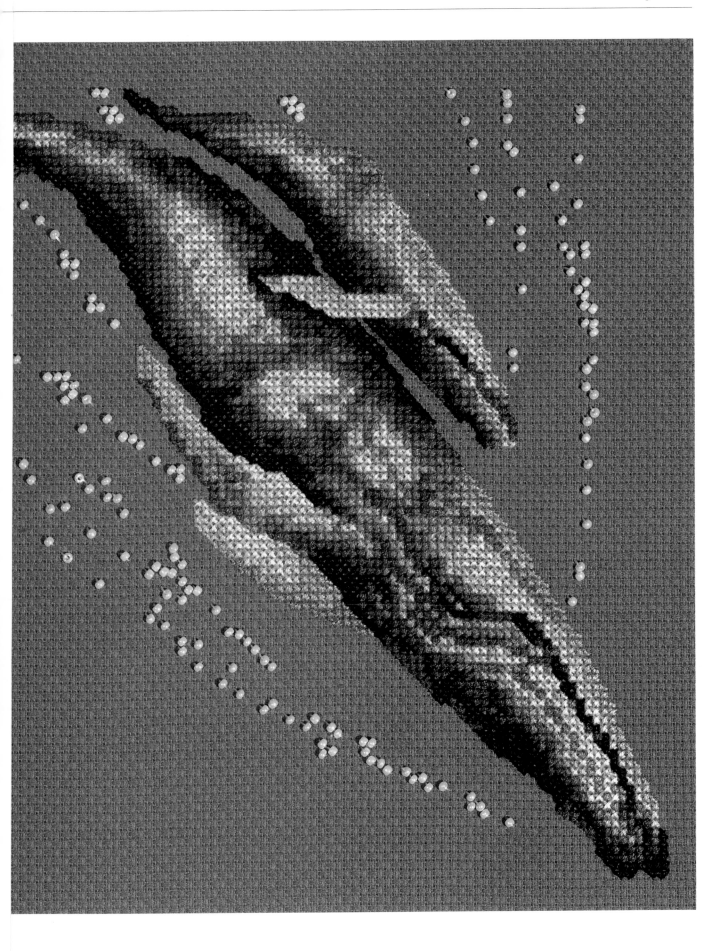

DISPLAY IT

Each of the individual motifs that make up the Ocean Life opening design could be stitched separately to make a lovely set of pictures for a bathroom. The hermit crab could be stitched on a small square of Aida, edged with a complementary coloured bias binding and stitched onto a towel. Stitched up in a larger count it would also make a super bath mat. The turtle and mackerel designs could be inset into a box (shown on page 2), stitched on a complementary coloured Aida, such as a parchment colour. It is also possible to stitch a single turtle, which can then be used for mugs and cards. Pick the most complete turtle in the design; this may have a foot missing but just take the missing part of the design from another turtle. The turtles are all the same, just over- and under-laid, turned and reversed to make up the design.

POLAR WILDLIFE

A LOVELY GREY SEAL with soft, appealing eyes just about to pull herself from the foaming waves onto the shore is the central design for my polar collection. The female grey seal may live for about thirty-five years and the male for about twenty-five. Surrounding her is a mother polar bear with cub and a wonderful orca leaping out of the sea into the air. An arctic fox in his winter white coat, a mother and baby common seal and two emperor penguins also feature in the design. Each of the motifs can be stitched on their own or framed as small pictures, like the orca on page 97. There are more ideas on how to use the designs in Display It, on page 114.

There are also three additional designs in this collection: a fabulous head and shoulder study of a wolf; a charming group of Adélie penguins diving off an icy ledge into the sea; and lastly a superb mountain hare on a snow-laden mountain landscape, his snowy coat perfectly complemented by icy blue Aida.

Polar Wildlife

STITCH IT

Fabric:	*28 count dove grey Zweigart Brittney 59 x 59cm (23 x 23in)*
Threads:	*DMC stranded cotton (floss)*
Stitch count:	*209 x 209*
Design size:	*38 x 38cm (15 x 15in) approx*
Stitches:	*Whole cross stitch, three-quarter cross stitch, backstitch, French knots, long stitch*

Prepare your fabric for work and mark the centre point (see Workbox). Follow the chart on pages 98–101, using two strands of stranded cotton (floss) for cross stitch, worked over two threads of evenweave fabric.

Work the backstitch in one strand of 310 for the main seal's eyes, the mother seal and cub mouths and the arctic fox's eye. Work the French knots in one strand of white for the eye highlights on the emperor penguins and the arctic fox.

Work the long stitches in one strand of white for the main seal's whiskers and eyebrows (shown in black on the chart).

Mount and frame your picture to complete or see Display It, page 114.

POLAR COLLECTION THREAD LIST

1 skein each DMC stranded cotton (floss)

3799	v. dk pewter grey	762	v. lt pearl grey	841	lt beige brown	3032	med mocha brown
712	cream	503	med blue green	676	lt golden sand	742	lt tangerine
413	dk silver grey	ecru	ecru	842	v. lt beige brown	3782	lt mocha brown
3866	beige	3813	lt blue green	677	v. lt golden sand	743	med yellow
317	silver grey	3371	black brown	543	ultra v. lt beige brown	3033	v. lt mocha brown
822	lt beige grey	504	lt blue green	746	off white	744	pale yellow
414	dk silver grey	838	v. dk beige brown	3862	dk brown	945	tawny
500	v. dk blue green	420	dk hazelnut brown	918	dk red copper	745	lt pale yellow
318	lt silver grey	839	dk beige brown	3863	med brown	738	v. lt tawny
501	dk blue green	3828	hazelnut brown	740	tangerine	3823	v. pale yellow
415	silver grey	840	med beige brown	3864	lt brown	739	ultra v. lt tan
502	blue green	729	med golden sand	741	med tangerine		

2 skeins each DMC stranded cotton (floss)

310	black

3 skeins each DMC stranded cotton (floss)

blanc	white

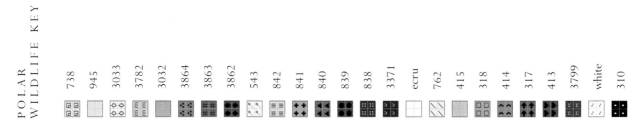

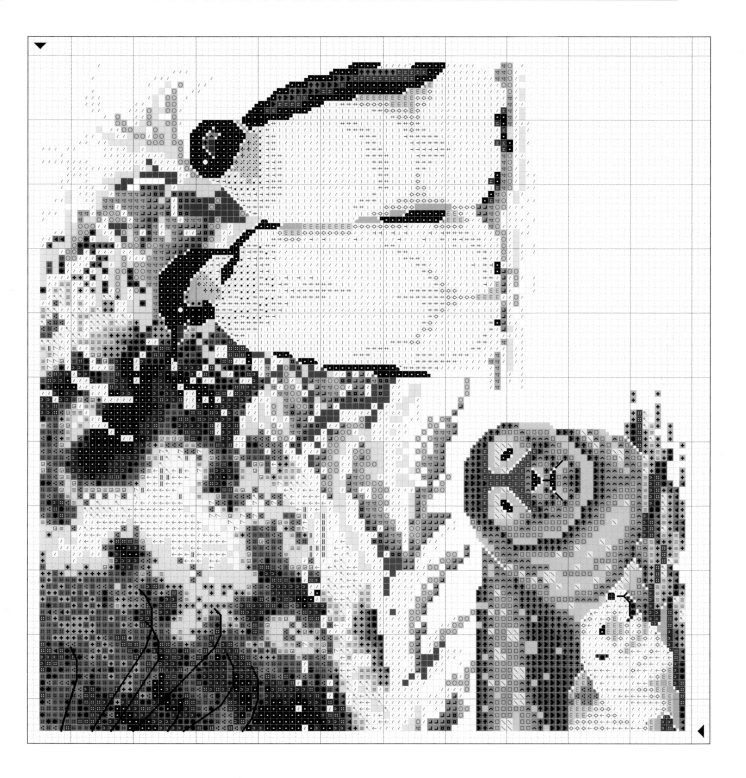

3823 745 744 743 742 741 740 918 746 677 676 729 3828 420 504 3813 503 502 501 500 822 3866 712 739

Wolf

ONE OF THE MOST GORGEOUS OF ANIMALS, the wolf is making a comeback in many regions of the world, from North America to Ethiopia. Only a few lucky people have ever come face to face with this wonderful beast, but we all know him through our pet dog, stories and legends. This head and shoulder picture, with the piercing eyes and luscious coat, is worked to perfection using subtle shading and shown most dramatically when worked on black Aida.

STITCH IT

Fabric:	*14 count black Aida 43 x 35cm (17 x 14in)*
Threads:	*DMC stranded cotton (floss) (see thread list page 113)*
Stitch count:	*150 x 106*
Design size:	*27 x 19cm (10¾ x 7½in) approx*
Stitches:	*Whole cross stitch, three-quarter cross stitch*

Prepare your fabric for work and mark the centre point (see Workbox). Follow the chart on pages 104/105, using two strands of stranded cotton (floss) for all cross stitch.

Mount and frame your picture to complete or see Display It, page 114.

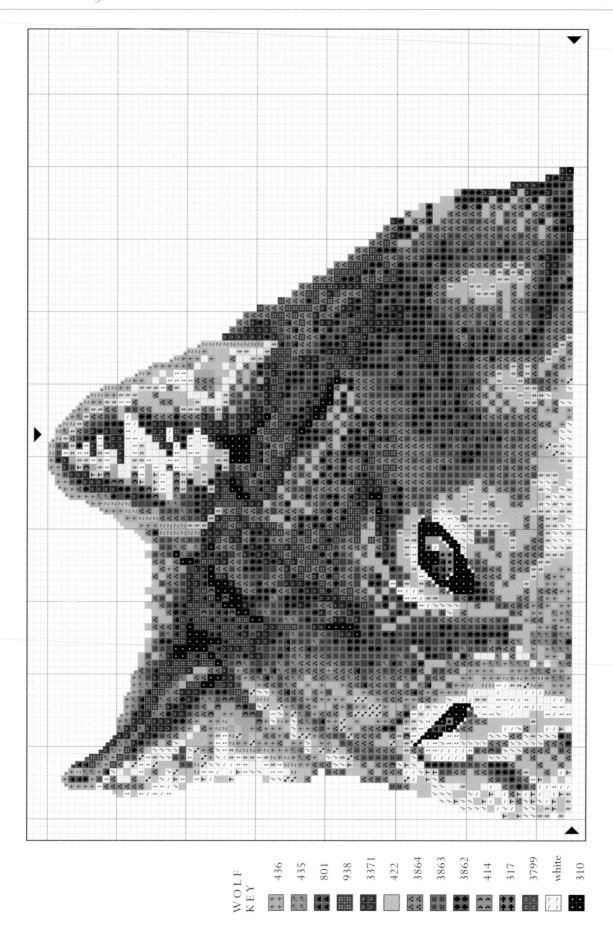

WOLF
KEY

436 435 801 938 3371 422 3864 3863 3862 414 317 3799 white 310

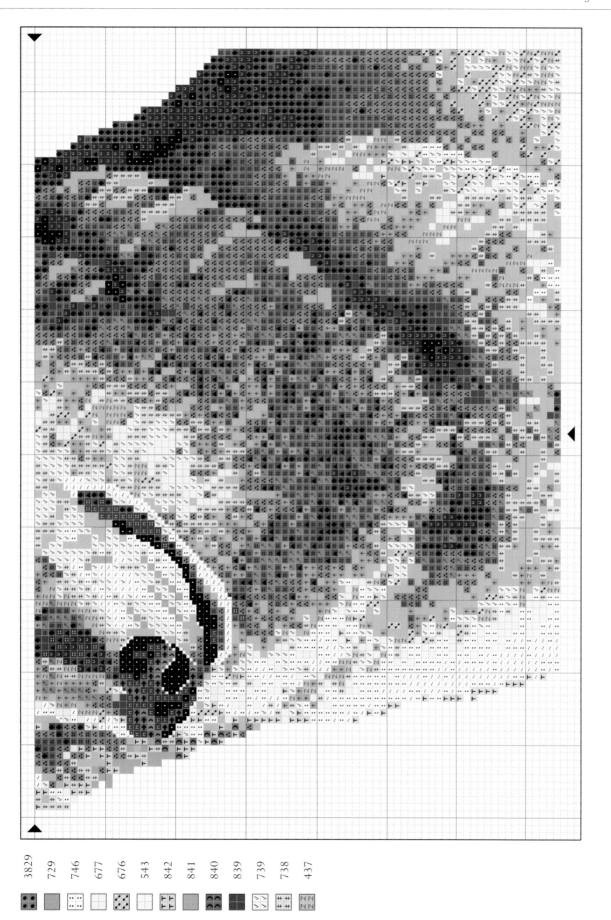

3829 729 746 677 676 543 842 841 840 839 739 738 437

Adélie Penguins

THERE ARE SEVENTEEN SPECIES of penguins.
Only six of these breed in Antarctica, and only
two of these six are exclusive to Antarctic –
the emperor penguin and the Adélie
penguin. The Adélie is the most common of
all penguins in Antarctica and for this design
I have depicted some launching themselves
from an icy ledge into the sea to feed on krill.
On land, they find walking arduous and
instead opt to toboggan, but once in the water
they are much more agile.

STITCH IT

Fabric:	*14 count sky blue Aida* *51 x 38cm (20 x 15in)*
Threads:	*DMC stranded cotton (floss)* *(see thread list page 113)*
Stitch count:	*170 x 98*
Design size:	*31 x 18cm (12 x 7in) approx*
Stitches:	*Whole cross stitch, three-quarter cross stitch, backstitch*

Prepare your fabric for work and mark the
centre point (see Workbox). Follow the chart
on pages 108/109, using two strands of
stranded cotton (floss) for all cross stitch
throughout. Work the backstitch for the eyes
with one strand of 762.

Mount and frame your picture to complete
or see Display It, page 114.

ADELIE
PENGUINS
KEY

3768	939	932	413	415	3033	898
924	928	931	3799	318	3782	918
white	927	930	3753	414	3032	3778
310	926	3750	3752	317	762	758

Mountain Hare

ALTHOUGH SIMILAR IN APPEARANCE to a rabbit, the hare can be distinguished by three chief points – it is bigger, has longer ears and much longer hind legs. In the winter the mountain hare's coat turns white. Unlike rabbits, they live solitary lives and never burrow. They spend their days lying in a hollow in the grass, which are known as forms, as they retain the shape of the animal's body. The young are born with their eyes open and can use their legs from birth. Each one makes its own form and is visited by the doe to be suckled. My design shows a hare just changing his coat, with a hint of a mountain range behind him.

STITCH IT

Fabric:	*14 count sky blue Aida 38 x 43cm (15 x 17in)*
Threads:	*DMC stranded cotton (floss) (see thread list page 113)*
Stitch count:	*100 x 123*
Design size:	*18 x 22cm (7 x 8¾in) approx*
Stitches:	*Whole cross stitch, three-quarter cross stitch, backstitch*

Prepare your fabric for work and mark the centre point (see Workbox). Follow the chart on page 112, using two strands of stranded cotton (floss) for all cross stitch. Work the backstitch in two strands of black 310 stranded cotton (floss) for the eye outline.

Mount and frame your picture to complete or see Display It, page 114.

	869		677		644		3781		3042		3826	MOUNTAIN
	801		676		642		783		3041		975	HARE KEY
	938		422		640		781		928		469	
	white		3828		3790		780		927		936		414
	310		420		746		822		926		3743		413

WOLF THREAD LIST
1 skein each DMC stranded cotton (floss)

310	black	839	dk beige brown	3864	lt grey brown	746	off white
437	lt tan	414	dk silver grey	543	v. lt beige brown	801	dk coffee brown
blanc	white	840	med beige brown	422	lt hazelnut brown	729	med golden sand
738	lt tan	3862	dk grey brown	676	lt golden sand	435	lt golden brown
3799	dk pewter grey	841	lt beige brown	3371	black brown	3829	dk golden sand
739	lt tan	3863	med grey brown	677	lt golden sand	436	tan
317	silver grey	842	lt beige brown	938	dk coffee brown		

ADELIE PENGUINS THREAD LIST
1 skein each DMC stranded cotton (floss)

924	v. dk grey green	318	lt silver grey	930	dk antique blue	3778	lt terra cotta
413	dk silver grey	928	v. lt grey green	3782	lt mocha brown	3753	ultra v. lt antique blue
3768	dk grey green	415	silver grey	931	med antique blue	918	dk red copper
317	silver grey	939	v. dk navy blue	3033	v. lt mocha brown	3799	v. dk pewter grey
926	med grey green	762	v. lt pearl grey	932	lt antique blue	898	v. dk coffee brown
414	dk silver grey	3750	v. dk antique blue	758	v. lt terra cotta		
927	lt grey green	3032	med mocha brown	3752	v. lt antique blue		

2 skeins each DMC stranded cotton (floss)

310	black	blanc	white

MOUNTAIN HARE THREAD LIST
1 skein each DMC stranded cotton (floss)

310	black	926	med grey green	677	v. lt golden sand	3826	dk rust
780	ultra v. dk topaz	420	dk hazelnut brown	3743	v. lt silver plum	644	med beige grey
blanc	white	927	lt grey green	746	off white	413	dk silver grey
781	v. dk topaz	3828	hazelnut brown	936	v. dk avocado green	822	lt beige grey
938	ultra dk coffee brown	928	v. lt grey green	3790	ultra dk beige grey	414	dk silver grey
783	med topaz	422	lt hazelnut brown	469	avocado green		
801	dk coffee brown	3041	dk silver plum	640	v. dk beige grey		
3781	dk mocha brown	676	lt golden sand	975	v. dk rust		
869	v. dk hazelnut brown	3042	lt silver plum	642	dk beige grey		

DISPLAY IT

Here are just a few suggestions for displaying the
animals featured in this chapter. The Polar Wildlife
opening design could be stitched as a complete
picture or would make a wonderful cushion (see
page 124 for instructions). Each of the smaller
motifs could be used on its own as a small picture.
The emperor penguins could be inset into a mug or
card or made up into a pincushion, using a
complementary backing fabric and finishing the
edges with bias binding or braid. The orca could be
stitched with white beads used instead of cross
stitch to emphasize the water droplets falling from
the fins. Parts of the leaping penguins design could
be used for a very small picture, using only the
three penguins in the foreground. The wolf would
look super if stitched in wool (yarn) on canvas as a
wall hanging (see pages 119 and 126 for advice).

WORKBOX

This chapter gives you all the information you'll need to produce perfect cross stitch embroidery and successfully recreate the projects in this book. There is advice on materials and equipment, embroidery techniques, stitches and making up methods.

MATERIALS AND EQUIPMENT

The materials and equipment needed for successful cross stitch are minimal. This section describes the basics you will need to complete the projects in this book.

Fabrics

Most of the designs in this book have been worked on Aida fabric which is stitched over *one* block. In the main, the size used is 14 blocks or threads to one inch (2.5cm), often called 14 count. Some designs use an evenweave fabric such as linen which should be worked over *two* threads. The same design stitched on fabrics of different counts will work up as different sizes. The larger the count (e.g. 18 count), the more threads per inch (2.5cm), therefore the smaller the finished design, and vice versa. Each project lists the type of fabric used, giving the thread count and fabric name, which should be quoted when purchasing goods. All DMC threads and fabrics are available from good needlework shops (see also Suppliers).

Threads

If you want your designs to look exactly the same as those shown in the photographs, you need to use the colours and threads listed for each project. The threads used in this book are DMC stranded cotton (floss). On some of the projects I have suggested that they could be stitched with tapestry wool (yarn) instead.

It is advisable to keep threads tidy and manageable and thread organisers and project cards are ideal for this purpose. Cut the threads to equal lengths and loop them into project cards with the thread shade code and colour key symbol written at the side. This will prevent threads from becoming tangled and the shade codes being lost.

STRANDED COTTON (FLOSS) This is the most widely used embroidery thread and is available in hundreds of colour shades, including silver and gold metallic. It is made from six strands twisted together to form a thick thread, which can be used whole or split into thinner strands. The type of fabric used will determine how many strands of thread you use: most of the designs in this book use two strands for cross stitch and one strand for backstitch.

TAPESTRY WOOL (YARN) DMC wool is a matt, hairy yarn made from 100 per cent wool. It is made from short fibres twisted together to make a thick single thread which cannot be split. Designs using tapestry wool are usually worked on a canvas using one or two strands. A wide selection of colours is available, with shades tending to be slightly duller than for stranded cotton. There are conversion lists for colour matching from stranded cotton to tapestry yarn – ask at your needlework shop.

Needles

Stitch your designs using a tapestry needle which has a large eye and a blunt end to prevent damage to the fabric. Choose a size of needle that will slide easily through the holes of the fabric without distorting or enlarging them. If using beads to enhance a design you will need to use a beading needle, which is thinner and longer. You will probably find it easier to sew if you use a thimble, especially for canvas.

Scissors

You will need a sharp pair of embroidery scissors for cutting your embroidery threads and also a pair of good dressmaking scissors for cutting fabric.

Embroidery Frames

Your work will be easier to handle and stitches will be kept flat and smooth if you mount your fabric on to an embroidery hoop or frame, which will accommodate the whole design. Bind the outer ring of an embroidery hoop with a white bias tape to prevent it from marking the fabric. This will also keep the fabric taut and prevent it from slipping whilst you are working.

BASIC TECHNIQUES

The following techniques and tips will help you attain a professional finish by showing you how to prepare for work, work the stitches and care for your finished embroidery.

Preparing the Fabric

Spending a little time preparing your embroidery fabric for work is a good idea, helping to avoid mistakes and produce superior finished results.

FABRIC SIZES Start by making sure you are using the correct size of fabric. You can check this by looking at the stitch count (the number of stitches across the height and width of the design) and design size given with each project. Each project gives the finished size of a design when worked on the recommended fabric, together with the amount of fabric needed. The overall fabric size should be at least 8–10cm (3–4in) larger than the finished size of the design to allow for turnings or seam allowances when

mounting the work or making it up. To prevent fabric from fraying, machine stitch around the edges or bind with tape.

Measurements are given in metric with the imperial equivalent in brackets. Always use either metric or imperial – do not try to mix the two.

CENTRE POINT Starting your stitching from the centre point on the fabric ensures you will have enough fabric all round the design. To find the centre point, tack (baste) a row of stitches horizontally and vertically from the centre of each side of the fabric. These lines correspond to the arrows at the side of each chart and will cross at the centre point.

Using Charts and Keys

All the designs in this book use DMC embroidery fabrics and stranded cotton (floss). The colours and symbols shown on the chart key correspond to DMC shade codes. Each project lists the number of the skeins required for each thread colour together with a colour name, which is given for easy reference only – when purchasing threads, use the code numbers.

Each coloured square on the chart represents one complete cross stitch and some squares will also have a symbol. The colours and symbols correspond to those in the key at the side of each chart. A triangle in half a square represents a three-quarter cross stitch. French knots are indicated by a coloured dot – the project instructions specify what thread shade to use. The optional use of beads on some designs will be in the instructions and will also specify which colours they replace. Solid coloured lines indicate backstitch or long stitch – refer to the project instructions for details.

Small black arrows at the side of a chart indicate the centre, and by lining these up you will find the centre point. Some of the charts are spread over four pages with the colour key repeated on each double page. Small blue arrows on some of the charts indicate the cut-off line for the use of that design on another suggested project.

To prevent mistakes, work systematically so that you read the chart accurately. Constantly check your progress against the chart and count the stitches as you go. If your sight is poor you may find it helpful to enlarge a chart on a colour photocopier.

Adding Beads

Replacing a single thread colour with beads, such as seed heads or a whole section of a design, can really enhance the overall effect. For example, beads were used to replace all of the white cross stitch on the humpback whale and calf design.

To sew on beads, it is best to use a beading needle. Use matching thread and start with the needle at the right side of the fabric. Thread the bead over the needle and on to the thread, then attach it to the fabric by working a half cross stitch. All stitches should run in the same direction so that the beads lie in neat rows on the fabric.

Using Canvas

Many of the projects can be stitched on canvas with tapestry wool (yarn) if you prefer. This would make them perfect for more hard-wearing items such as doorstops, rugs and wall hangings. Ask at your needlework shop for a conversion list to change stranded cotton (floss) colours to wool (yarn). Remember when working on canvas that you will also need a complementary background wool colour to fill in the area around the design.

There is quite a large range of canvas, from lighter weight canvas used for embroidery to heavier canvas used for rugs. Canvas is basically of two types – tapestry and embroidery, and mono and interlock. Tapestry and embroidery canvases are ideal if the design has whole and three-quarter cross stitches or half and quarter cross stitches. Mono and interlock are ideal if the design has all whole cross stitch or half cross stitch.

When altering the count a design is stitched on, remember the design size will change so you need to work out carefully what size canvas is required. The count of any fabric or canvas will tell you how many stitches there are to every 2.5cm (1in). All of the projects have design sizes and stitch counts listed. Simply divide the stitch count by the fabric or canvas count and you will have the approximate size of the design area, without any allowance. Always be generous with the allowances, as you can trim the excess off. When working on canvas, add at least 13–15cm (5–6in) allowance all the way around a design.

Using Embroidery Bands

Embroidery bands, both Aida and evenweave types, are available in many colours, widths and stitch counts and are perfect for decorating many items, such as towels and linens. Aida bands have been used to decorate towels with the turtle and mackerel designs, as follows.

You will need a towel of a complementary colour, plus matching thread for stitching the band on to the towel. I chose a sand-coloured towel for the turtles and a blue-green for the fish. Measure the towel width and add 6mm (¼in) for turnings. Chose your band – I used a 2½in wide, 14 count white Aida band (with a 28 stitch width).

Use the portion of the turtle or mackerel chart on the left and up to the blue arrows (the cut-off line), which will give you a border width of 28 stitches. For a wider band move the cut-off line to the desired number of stitches. Begin stitching 6mm (¼in) from one end of the Aida band (which leaves enough for the turnings). Start at the top of the chart and work to the bottom, repeating the design as many times as necessary for the width of the towel.

When the embroidery is complete, turn the 6mm (¼in) turning ends under, pin, tack, (baste) and machine stitch onto the towel.

Using Waste Canvas

Waste canvas will allow you to work a design on a textured fabric such as fleece or towelling. It is available in various counts and is used just like Aida. It has blue lines running through it to mark off every five blocks making it easier to count stitches.

The waste canvas is tacked over your chosen fabric and is used as a temporary stitching surface, which is then removed to leave the completed design on the fabric.

To use waste canvas, cut a piece at least 5cm (2in) larger than your design. Lay the canvas over the base fabric so the blue lines run vertically along the fabric grain. Pin and tack (baste) in place (Fig 1) and mark the centre.

Fig 1

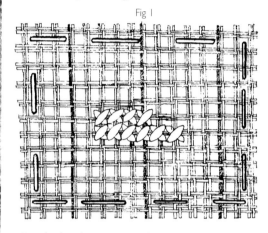

Stitch the design over the waste canvas following the project instructions for the cross stitch. When working, try to ensure that the corners of each stitch share the hole with the previous stitch in the base fabric as this will give a neater finished effect.

When the stitching is complete, remove the tacking (basting) threads, and trim away the excess waste canvas close to the cross stitches. Using a pair of tweezers carefully pull out the vertical threads of the waste canvas – the remaining horizontal threads can then be easily removed (Fig 2). If the waste canvas threads prove stubborn to remove it may help to slightly dampen them.

When all the waste canvas threads have been completely removed, press the embroidery from the wrong side, then add any backstitches, French knots or beads to complete your design.

Fig 2

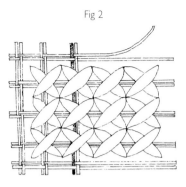

Washing and Pressing Embroidery

If your work has become grubby during stitching, gently hand wash in warm water using a mild liquid detergent. Use a soft nail brush to remove any stubborn marks, rinse in clean water, place the damp fabric on a clean white towel and leave to dry on a flat surface. Do not iron directly on your work as this will flatten the stitches and spoil the finished effect. Lay the work face down on a clean, white towel, cover with a clean, fine cloth and press.

THE STITCHES

Cross stitch embroidery is a simple and straightforward technique and the following section shows you how to work all the stitches used in the book. When following the stitch instructions, please note that stitching is over one block of Aida fabric or two threads of evenweave fabric.

Starting and Finishing Thread

To start off your first length of thread, make a knot at one end and push the needle through to the back of the fabric, about 3cm (1¼in) from your starting point, leaving the knot on the right side. Stitch towards the knot, securing the thread at the back of the fabric as you go (Fig 3). When the thread is secure, cut off the knot.

Fig 3

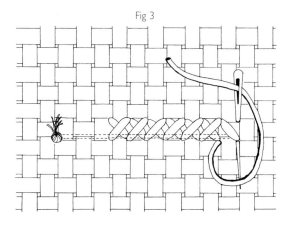

To finish off a thread or start new threads, simply weave the thread into the back of several worked stitches (Fig 4).

Fig 4

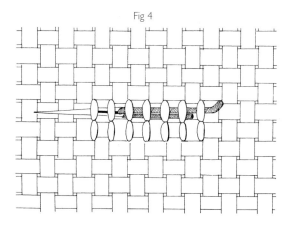

Backstitch

Backstitch is indicated on the charts by a solid coloured line. It is worked around areas of completed cross stitches to add definition or on top of stitches to add detail.

To work backstitch, pull the needle through the hole in the fabric at 1 (Fig 5), and then push back through at 2. For the next stitch, pull the needle through at 3, push to the back at 1, and then repeat the process to make the next stitch. This will give you short stitches at the front of your work and longer stitches at the back. If working backstitch on an evenweave fabric such as Zweigart Brittney, work each stitch over two threads.

Fig 5

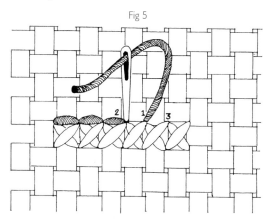

Cross Stitch

Each coloured square on the chart represents one complete cross stitch. Cross stitch is worked in two easy stages. Start by working one diagonal stitch over one block of Aida or two threads of evenweave, then work a second diagonal stitch

Fig 6

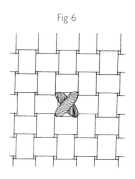

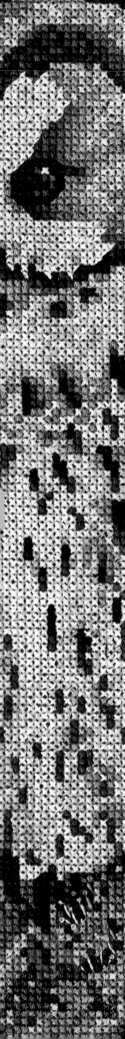

over the first stitch, but in the opposite direction to form a cross (Fig 6).

Cross stitches can also be worked in rows if you have a large area to cover. Work a row of half cross stitches in one direction and then work back in the opposite direction with the diagonal stitches to complete each cross. The upper stitches of all the crosses should lie in the same direction to produce a neat effect (Fig 7).

Fig 7

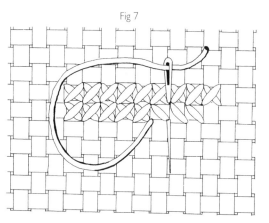

Quarter Cross Stitch

If you chose to work a design on a double mesh canvas using wool (yarn), a quarter cross stitch should be used instead of a three-quarter cross stitch. So, where a three-quarter cross stitch is shown on the chart, use a quarter stitch instead.

To work a quarter stitch, start at one corner of the canvas mesh and work in the same direction as any half stitches, but insert the needle at the corner of the square (Fig 8).

Half Cross Stitch

This stitch is also used if you chose to work a design on canvas in tapestry wool (yarn), replacing whole cross stitches with half stitches. A half cross stitch is simply one half of a cross stitch, with the diagonal facing the

Fig 8

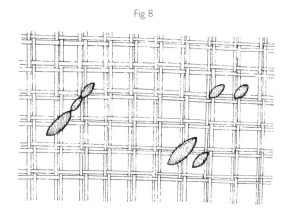

same way as the upper stitches of each complete cross stitch (Fig 8).

Three-quarter Cross Stitch

A small, coloured square taking up a quarter of a chart square represents a three-quarter cross stitch. Forming fractional stitches such as three-quarter cross stitches is less accurate on Aida than on an evenweave or linen fabric because the centre of the Aida block needs to be pierced (Fig 9).

Fig 9

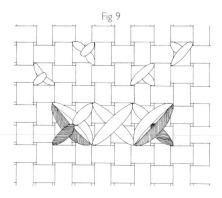

Work the first half of a cross stitch in the normal way, then work the second diagonal stitch in the opposite corner but insert the needle at the centre of the cross, forming three-quarters of the complete stitch. A square showing two smaller coloured squares in opposite corners indicates that two of these three-quarter stitches will have to be made back to back.

French Knots

These are small knots, indicated on the chart by a small coloured dot, which are used to add detail, for example, as eye highlights. Some designs, such as the tawny owl use large areas of French knots and more than one colour.

To work a French knot, bring the needle through to the front of the fabric, just above the point where you want the stitch placed. Wind the thread once around the needle and holding the twisted thread firmly, insert the needle a little away from its starting position (Fig 10).

Fig 10

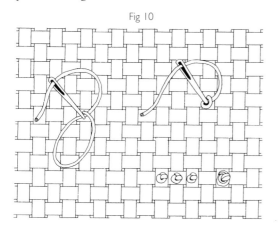

Two tips for working French knots: never rush them and never go back into the same point where your thread came up or your knot will just pull through to the back.

Long Stitch

Long stitches are used to work whiskers and eyebrow hairs and some plant stems and are indicated on charts by a straight, solid coloured line – often in a different, easier-to-see colour. Refer to the instructions for the actual colour. Work long stitches on top of the completed stitched design.

To work long stitch, pull the needle

through the fabric at the point indicated on the chart, then push through at the other end, to make a long stitch on top of the fabric. Repeat for the next stitch, carrying the thread across the back of the fabric to the next starting point (Fig 11).

Fig 11

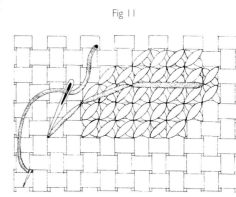

STITCHING TIPS

◆ Steam press your embroidery fabric before stitching to remove any stubborn creases.

◆ Mount fabric onto an embroidery frame or hoop to keep stitches smooth and flat.

◆ Work cross stitches with the top diagonals all facing in the same direction.

◆ Thread up lengths of several colours of stranded cotton (floss) into needles, and arrange these at the side of your work by shade code number or by key reference.

◆ Work the designs from the centre outwards, or split them into workable sections such as quarters. On larger designs, first work the main subject and then complete the background and surrounding designs.

◆ When taking threads across the back of a design, weave the thread through the back of existing stitches to avoid any ugly lines showing through on the right side.

◆ Use short lengths of thread, about 30cm (12in), to reduce any knotting and tangling.

◆ Check your work constantly against the chart to avoid making mistakes.

◆ For a smooth piece of work without any lumps or bumps, avoid using knots at the back, and cut off any excess threads as short as possible.

◆ Keep your work clean by packing it away in its own clean plastic bag to prevent any accidents.

MAKING UP

One of the reasons why cross stitch is so popular, apart from being so easy to work, is that the designs are simple to adapt and use in different ways. Merely by changing the material used – the fabric, the thickness or type of thread or the background colour – a design can be transformed, and examples of this are given throughout the book. The following section describes how to make up the embroideries as illustrated in the book. Most of the designs have been mounted and framed as pictures but there are dozens of other ideas for making up given throughout the Display It pages. When making up any item, a 1.5cm (⅝in) seam allowance has been used unless otherwise stated.

Mounting and Framing

It really is easiest and best to take larger pictures to a professional framer, who will be able to stretch the fabric correctly and cut any surrounding mounts accurately. If, however, you choose to do the mounting and framing yourself you will need a box for cutting mitred edges on frames, some panel pins, a suitable saw, some hardboard (or thick card) and mount board. When choosing mount board and framing, it is best to take your finished work with you, to get the best idea of what the end result will be.

Mount your embroidery onto some thin hardboard or card and fasten in place by lacing it around the card or by stapling it. Decide on the frame size you require and carefully cut your frame pieces to the correct size, then panel pin them together. Using a mount cutter (which is by far the easiest) or a craft or Stanley knife, cut your mount board to the required depth. Place the mount board into the frame, then the embroidery. Finally, cut hardboard to size for the backing and wedge in with metal clips or tape in place.

Using Ready-made Items

Many of the projects in the book can be displayed in ready-made items such as trinket boxes, stools, mugs, teapot stands, coasters, cards and small frames or flexi-hoops (see Suppliers). Smaller pieces of embroidery can be backed with lightweight iron-on interfacing to prevent the fabric wrinkling, and then mounted following the manufacturer's instructions.

Making a Cushion with a Frill

Many of the designs in the book can be made up into gorgeous cushions. The instructions which follow are for a 38 x 38cm (15 x 15in) cushion with a frilled edge but the principles can be applied to any size. You will need a cushion pad, matching sewing thread and sufficient fabric for backing and making a frill.

For the cushion front, carefully cut away the excess embroidery fabric, leaving a square with a 1.5cm (⅝in) seam allowance. For the cushion backs, cut two pieces of cotton fabric 25.5 x 38cm (10 x 15in). Take each rectangle and hem along one long edge. To make the frill, cut enough 12cm (4¾in) wide strips along the length of the cotton fabric to give a finished length of 2.9m (3⅛yd). With right sides facing, stitch the fabric strips together along the short edges to form a circle. Press seams open. Fold the strip in half so that the long edges meet, enclosing the raw edges of the short seams, then press (Fig 12).

Run two rows of gathering threads along the raw edges of the frill fabric, then pull up the thread until the frill is the right length, distributing the gathers evenly. With the embroidered fabric facing outwards, place the frill around the outer edge of the cushion front, so raw edges face outwards. Distribute the gathers evenly, then pin, tack (baste) and machine stitch in place.

Lay the embroidered fabric face upwards on a flat surface. With right sides down, lay the two rectangles of the cushion back on top of the front so that all the raw edges match and the hemmed edges overlap at the centre. Pin, tack (baste) and then machine stitch along the stitching line and through all layers of fabric. Neaten the raw edges, then turn the cover through to the right side and insert a cushion pad.

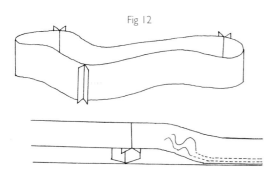

Fig 12

Making a Cushion with a Braid Edge and Tassels

This type of cushion makes an elegant statement and could be used to display many of the designs, including the large collages such as the Safari Collection and also smaller designs like the little bee-eaters. A

pincushion can also be made following the same principles. You will need a cushion pad, matching sewing thread, sufficient fabric for backing and enough thick furnishing braid to go around your cushion. Follow the instructions for making the frilled cushion, above, but omit the frill.

After making the cushion cover, turn it through to the right side. Measure the length of the cushion edges, then cut lengths of braid to the same measurements, adding 10cm (4in) to each length. Hand stitch the braid along each edge, leaving equal lengths extending at each end. Pinch together the two lengths of braid extending from each corner, then use matching sewing thread to tightly bind them together. Secure the sewing thread with a knot, then fray the braid to make a tassel (Fig 13).

Fig 13

Making a Doorstop

Making work up as a doorstop is easy to do and would make a wonderful feature of such designs as the tawny owl and the puma. You will need medium-weight interfacing, cotton backing fabric, a quantity of wadding (batting) and some clean kitty litter or sawdust.

Back the embroidery with a medium-weight iron-on interfacing, following the manufacturer's instructions. Use a soft pencil to draw a line all around the design 1.5cm (⅝in) from the finished embroidery and cut away excess fabric along this line. Cut a piece of cotton backing fabric to the same shape.

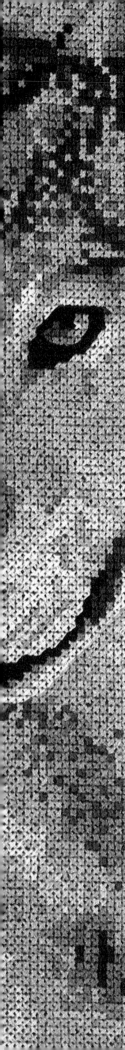

With right sides facing, place the front and back pieces together then pin and tack (baste) around the edges. Machine stitch the layers together, taking a 1.5cm (⅝in) seam allowance and leaving a 20cm (8in) gap along the bottom straight edge for turning.

Turn the doorstop through to the right side and almost fill with wadding (batting). Then, fill a sock with kitty litter or sawdust and tie a knot at the end. Insert the filled sock into the base of the doorstop then close the gap with slipstitches.

Making a Wall Hanging or Rug

Wall hangings and small rugs are lovely ways to display embroidery. Wall hangings can be stitched in either stranded cotton (floss) or wool (yarn). Rugs need to be more hard wearing and so need to be stitched on canvas with wool (yarn). See page 119 for tips on working with canvas.

To convert the wolf design into a wool wall hanging, I would suggest using a 10 count embroidery/tapestry canvas, as the design has three-quarter cross stitches. You can stitch it with one thread of tapestry wool (yarn) either in whole and three-quarter cross stitch or in half and quarter cross stitch.

The puma design would look wonderful stitched up as a rug, as it is worked using whole cross stitch. Use a 7 count mono or interlock canvas, whole cross stitch and two threads of tapestry wool (yarn).

EDGING RUGS AND WALL HANGINGS
The edges of the finished embroidered design will need to be neatened and

strengthened. Trim away excess canvas to within 10cm (4in) of the stitches. Fold the turnings to the back, leaving one hole showing and one thread running across the top of the fold, then stitch the turnings in place by stitching an overcast edging using two strands of the desired colour. Secure the thread at the back of the canvas, insert the needle into the hole nearest the embroidery stitches and pull to the front. The overcast thread should share a hole with the last stitch of the design. Take the needle to the back of the canvas and work the next stitch in the same way. Work one, two or three stitches in each hole to cover the canvas completely (Fig 14).

Fig 14

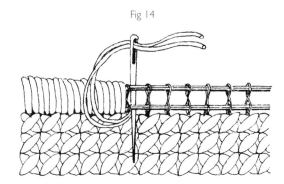

HANGING A WALL HANGING Either sew on curtain rings at intervals along the top on the wrong side, at a depth of 1½–2in (4–5cm), or make loops by cutting two 20cm (8in) strips of flat braid. Fold the strips in half to form a loop, then use sewing thread to hand stitch them in place at the back of the wall hanging at either end of the top edge. Slide a curtain rod or length of wooden dowelling through these to suspend it from the wall, from cup hooks or other suitable fastenings.

SUPPLIERS

If you should require any further information about products, catalogues, price lists or local stockists from any of the suppliers mentioned, contact them direct by post or phone. Remember to always include a stamped addressed envelope. If contacting them by phone, they will be able to tell you if there is any charge for the catalogue or price lists.

DMC Creative World

Pullman Road, Wigston, Leicester LE18 2DY. Tel: (0116) 281 1040. *For all threads, embroidery fabrics and beads used throughout the book, and for the name and address of your nearest DMC and Zweigart stockist.*

DMC threads are supplied in the USA by:
The DMC Corporation, South Hackensack Ave, Port Kearny, Building 10A, South Kearny, NJ 07032-4688. www.dmc-usa.com
Zweigart fabric is supplied in the USA by Joan Toggitt Ltd, 2 River View Drive, Somerset, NJ 08873-1139.
E-mail: info@zweigart.com
www.zweigart.com

Framecraft Miniatures Ltd

376 Summer Lane, Hockley, Birmingham B19 3QA.
Tel: (0121) 2120551.
For ready-made items for embroidery. Suppliers of the hexagonal teapot stand, coffeepot stand, mugs and cards.

Framecraft products are also supplied worldwide by:
Anne Brinkley Designs Inc,
761 Palmer Avenue, Holmdel, NJ 97733, USA.
Gay Bowles Sales Inc, PO Box 1060, Janesville, WI 53547, USA.
Ireland Needlecraft Pty Ltd, 4, 2–4 Keppel Drive, Hallam, Vic 3803, Australia.

Market Square (Warminster) Ltd

Wing Farm, Longbridge Deverill, Warminster, Wilts BA12 7DD.
Tel: 01985 841042.
Suppliers of the chest for the turtle design.

Sleepy Hollow

Duke House, Duke Street, Kingsbridge, Devon TQ7 1HU.
Tel: 01548 857949.
Suppliers of the smock tops for the zebra and elephant designs.

Vilene products were used on projects throughout the book. A selection of iron-on interfacings is available in major department stores and all good haberdashery shops (notions departments).

ACKNOWLEDGMENTS

A very special thank you to my husband Ian, for all his support, help and understanding while I worked on this book. Thank you also goes to Pops, who always reminds me how much I love my work when I'm feeling under pressure and over-worked, and to my mother and my two brothers, Nick and Edward, who are always there with advice and encouragement when I need it.

Thanks to Doreen Montgomery for her encouragement, advice and support from the outset of this book. Thank you also to the following people at David & Charles for their contributions and help with getting this book published: Cheryl Brown for her persuasion, encouragement and advice from the beginning; my editor Linda Clements for her invaluable help with the text; and also Ali Myer, Lisa Forrester and Sandra Pruski. Thanks to Jon Bouchier for the wonderful photography, and to David Lynch for the photograph on the back cover flap.

Thank you also to Cara Ackerman at DMC and Sarah Carlton-Gray at Framecraft Miniatures Ltd for their support. A huge thank you to John Parkes of Outpost Trading, who, as usual, had to rush my framing through at the last moment. Thank you to Sleepy Hollow for letting me use their wonderful smock tops for the zebra and elephant designs.

Index

Charts are in *italic*   Chapters headings in **bold**